D1450546

BEARS I HAVE KNOWN

Bob Murphy

RIVERBEND
PUBLISHING

Copyright © 2006 by Bob Murphy

Published by Riverbend Publishing, Helena, Montana.

Printed in the United States.

2 3 4 5 6 7 8 9 0 MG 10 09 08 07

ISBN 13: 978-1-931832-64-9
ISBN 10: 1-931832-64-1

Cataloging-in-Publication data is on file at the Library of Congress.

Riverbend Publishing
P.O. Box 5833
Helena, MT 59604
Toll-free: 1-866-787-2363
www.riverbendpublishing.com

Grizzly bear cover photo by JESSLEEPHOTOS.COM

Contents

BEAR ENVIRONS

BEARS have had a long exposure to humans in the national parks. Earlier generations of park managers and visitors struggled with the same fascination, amusement, fear, and a sense of responsibility that park bears still inspire today.

In recent years, extensive research, especially in Yellowstone National Park, has enhanced public understanding of the ecology of bears, creating a greater awareness of the many problems to be confronted. At the same time, public affection for bears has not diminished, and in many areas controversy has been generated, creating serious challenges to management.

We may look back and realize that over time our attitudes have changed, likely for the benefit of both humans and bears, and the total welfare of both may be enhanced.

EARLY ENCOUNTERS

IN early years in Yellowstone National Park, grizzly bears were not seen as especially dangerous. However, in 1916 there were three separate attacks made upon men in Yellowstone by grizzly bears. Chub Jones was chewed up and badly lacerated by a grizzly at the Sylvan Lake Camp in midsummer; on August 14 Ned Frost and Ed Jones were terribly injured by a grizzly at their campsite at Indian Pond on the north shore of Yellowstone Lake; and on September 7 Jack Welch, a teamster for the Army Quartermaster Corp, was so severely injured and torn up by a grizzly near Turbid Lake that he died at the Mammoth Hot Springs hospital and was buried at the post cemetery.

To amplify the serious nature of this fatality, Welch was sleeping under his freight wagon laden with hay and oats in company of a Mr. Devlin, while another helper was sleeping on top of the wagon. The grizzly first attacked Devlin, who threw his bedding and blankets at it and yelled to wake up Welch. Devlin then clambered to the top of the wagon while the grizzly circled the wagon and grabbed Welch, extracting him from his bedroll. The two men on top of the wagon threw a large, heavy, lunch box at the bear and began throwing hay bales at it. Welch started to climb on top of the wagon, whereupon the grizzly rushed in and pulled Welch to the ground. Again the discharge of hay bales frightened off the bear, but the grizzly returned, grabbing Welch a third time and this time terribly mangling his shoulder, rib area, and abdomen. Again, bales of hay tumbling onto the bear allowed his companions to get Welch on top of the wagon.

The Ned Frost—Ed Jones attack at Indian Pond had many of the same characteristics. Ned Frost later commented, "About midnight we were aroused by the most bloodcurdling yells I ever heard come from human kind. Raising myself in my bedroll, I saw there in the bright moonlight about fifteen feet away from me a huge grizzly. He had Jonsey, the cook, by the back and was shaking him, bed and all, as a terrier shakes a rat. Yelling at the top of my voice, as Shorty, the horse wrangler, was also doing, I threw my pillow. As the white mass landed in front of him, the bear flung Jonsey to the ground and started back. The grizzly caught site of me as I sat up in bed waving my arms over my head in a vain attempt to scare him. Throwing myself back and jerking the bedroll over me, I drew my knees up and held the covers over my head and throat. I felt his fangs rasping on the bones about my knees almost with the first impact. Time after time he hurled me, bed and all, through the air, always getting farther from the camp into dark shadows of the thick timber, while the voices of the yelling Shorty and Jonsey grew fainter and fainter.

"The covers were finally pulled from my head and the gleaming fangs and drooling jaws were within a foot and a half of my eyes. The hot breath had a very repugnant odor, which seemed to almost choke me. I wondered just how it was going to feel when he would finally lose his hold on my legs and sink his great teeth into my exposed throat. I remember thinking it wouldn't be a hard death, for if he would just get me by the neck everything would be over quickly.

"That I was alive today I attribute to a lucky fluke. After shaking and carrying me along several times, he finally got a mouthful of sleeping bag, and with a vicious shake threw me clear of the bag, like a potato out of a sack. Head over heels I went for several yards, landing under some low hanging jack pine branches. I grasped these, intending to climb the tree, but my lacerated knees refused to bear my weight, so I went hand over hand to the very top, you may be sure, and the wonder was I was not going yet.

"The bear was still looking for me in the bed. By this time Shorty has made a dash for the night horse which was staked nearby. Jonsey, still yelling, upset the stove and table, with all the dishes in camp. With all the racket and disturbance, the old boy shambled off into the timber. The minute he was gone, Shorty beat it to the automobile camp and within twenty minutes we were on the way to the Lake Hotel. In less than an hour, two doctors and a nurse were working on us. Jonsey had four places in his back stitched up, and his face was sort of smeared sideways a bit where old Bruin had stomped on it. I had six wounds in my legs sewed up. In one the main artery, the size of a lead pencil, was exposed for two inches, but not ruptured. If it had been, I should have bled to death in minutes."

Ned Frost was nationally known for guiding big game hunting parties and summer fishing excursions out of Cody, Wyoming, area. On this trip he was returning from a trip down in Jackson Hole via the east shore of Yellowstone Lake.

As a result of these three encounters and others that followed, many people, including park managers, were shocked into an awareness of the unpredictability of the grizzly bear, and they made more realistic evaluations.

JOSEPH (FRENCHY) DURET

FRENCHY Duret owned a ranch on Slough Creek five miles north of the Yellowstone boundary and had set out traps for bears. Early on June 12, 1922, after visiting his traps, he returned to his ranch and told his wife he had caught a large grizzly bear. He took his rifle and left about 10 a.m. to go kill the bear. Nothing being heard from him, a search was started that afternoon and continued the next day. About 8 p.m. on the 13th, a park ranger found Duret's body, badly torn and mangled. Apparently he had crawled nearly 1.5 miles after escaping the bear.

The trap was found about 1.5 miles outside the park, and there were signs of a severe struggle. One cartridge had been fired from Frenchy's Winchester rifle. It was assumed that the enraged bear made a lunge, either before or after the shot, broke the trap's chain, sprang on Duret and mauled his body. There was nothing to indicate that Duret's shot wounded the bear and it may have missed altogether. The bear escaped, carrying the heavy trap with him, although efforts were made to find and kill the bear.

While Duret's death occurred on the 12th of June, it was not until the 14th that National Park Service administrative personnel learned of the event. It so happened that on the morning of the 14th, Superintendent Horace Albright, in

11

company with Chief Buffalo Keeper Bob Lacombe and Chief Park Ranger Sam Woodring, were inspecting the Slough Creek Hay Ranches. When riding on horseback between the termination of the automobile road and the Lower Slough Ranch, they were met by Assistant Buffalo Keeper Peck Hutchings, who was hurrying out on horseback to tell them of the Duret's death. All the party proceeded at a fast gait to the Upper Slough Creek Ranch, where they met Mrs. Duret and arranged for the burial of her husband in accordance with her wishes.

Arriving at the Duret Ranch, they removed some boards from the barn roof in order to make a coffin. Ranger Dehnhoff and Assistant Buffalo Keeper Hutchings, who had found the body, buried it on the 15th and read over it some verses from a Bible and said a prayer. The gravesite was approximately one mile southwest of the Duret Ranch, among some pine trees. In accordance with Mrs. Duret's wishes, Albright had the grave adorned with a white painted enclosure and a panel describing what happened. In later years a very large brown sign with routed white letters was installed, describing the character of Frenchy Duret and the accident that caused his death. Today the sight may be visited by park visitors or other travelers, a very attractive sight in the midst of the Absaroka Mountains. It may induce them to recount the character of the man and the tragedy that befell him.

UNFORTUNATE INCIDENTS

IN dealing with bear management problems, we many times learn by our mistakes, and at other times we become totally aware of mistakes made by others. The latter, unfortunately, includes incidents of severe injury or even death by a bear attack. Many adhere to the conviction that bear behavior, especially by grizzly bears, is unpredictable. However, when encountering bears there are precautions that provide a degree of safety that have been ignored or were unknown by persons so engaged. There is a definite fine line between safe observation and potential confrontation.

Situations vary in what may cause a grizzly bear to bluff charge a human or to continue the charge with obvious intent to harm or kill the object of their concern. In a majority of incidents, the degree of threat the intruder presents to the grizzly bear is what makes the difference.

In 1945 I had a crew of young men rebuilding the telephone line from near Turbid Lake to the Pelican Creek Patrol Cabin north of Yellowstone Lake. The work entailed removing old deteriorated poles, erecting new poles, and re-hanging the telephone line. I was using a saddle horse and a harnessed horse to drag the new poles and remove the old ones.

One early morning I rode out on a ridge along the phone line, looking down on Pelican Creek. Immediately I spotted a grizzly bear with two cubs along the creek about

250 yards below. When the mother grizzly spotted me, she went nuts! She tore up the landscape, raced around in circles, and knocked one cub into the creek. She was in a real rage, finally driving the cubs up the hill to my northeast toward the forest. She paused within 200 yards of my position, venting her alarm and discontent.

In the next two weeks we encountered this same mother and cubs several times in the early morning down on the creek. One time it was two or three young men digging holes for the telephone poles. Again the mother grizzly became enraged, tearing up vegetation, pushing the cubs around, voicing her discontent, and appearing highly concerned. As the workers remained silent and motionless, she moved her cubs up the hill into the nearby forest. On about the fifth encounter she merely looked in our direction and exhibited no real alarm. She gradually moved away upstream and lingered for nearly a half-hour before seeking refuge in the forest. Thus, she no longer regarded us as a significant threat and did not exhibit evidence of any appreciable alarm.

In June 1977, Barry Gilbert from Utah State College and a graduate student, Bruce Hastings, started a contract with Yellowstone National Park to research grizzly bear behavior. The project would be primarily directed at how grizzlies and people interact in the wild. Would they attack or bluff charge a human trespasser? What factors would trigger an attack? What conditions might prompt a grizzly to run away?

Their initial venture required backpacking into Bighorn Pass, a 9,200-foot saddle in the Gallatin Mountain Range in northwestern Yellowstone. This was a remote area with little visitor travel and quite attractive to grizzly bears. After camping overnight, the next morning they observed a mother grizzly and three cubs foraging in a basin nearly one mile away. Also, a lone bear, probably a boar, was in the immediate area and was observed approaching the family group a couple of times, whereby the mother grizzly charged him, driving him away. There were snow banks on some of the north slopes. A few elk were grazing on southern exposures. The wind was blowing very hard. The grizzly with her cubs wandered into some alpine cover and out of sight.

This was the first bear project for these men, as Gilbert's graduate studies had focused mostly on deer. Grizzly bears in the field were a new experience. The men wanted to observe the grizzlies more closely, so they took off up a long, spur ridge known as Crowfoot Ridge. This was alpine country with scattered alpine fir, white bark pine, shrubs, and grasses. Along the steep slope, Hastings moved some distance away to relieve himself.

Gilbert said he would continue ahead to the top of the ridge and over the top. Gilbert was walking fast into the strong wind but moved carefully over the top. "I cleared the skyline and dropped down, moving fast," he later recounted. He nearly ran into the mother grizzly he estimated at 40 yards away.

That's when the grizzly spotted him. The bear immediately charged, roaring as she ran toward him. Gilbert attempted to put some distance between them and ran as fast as he could. He made only a few steps before the bear was on him. It grabbed his leg, and as he went down, the grizzly tore off the back of his scalp. He then jammed his arms in its mouth, receiving a few bites there. "Then it just dropped its teeth and pulled away the side of my face. I could feel the cheekbone breaking off." One canine tooth punctured his left eye, destroying it forever and opening up the sinus cavity, gouging deep enough to touch the brain. Flesh from his forehead was peeled off, his nose was torn away and so were his ears.

Hastings was just finishing his business in the woods when he heard something odd. He picked up his pack and moved forward. The wind was blowing very hard so he couldn't be sure what he had heard. After a few steps forward he saw the bear, a chocolate-colored grizzly. "I wasn't sure what to do," he later said. Standing behind a small tree he shouted in a low tone, "Ha!" The bear lifted its head and as Hastings moved forward and looked again, the bear bolted for the horizon. Gilbert was lying in a pool of his own blood but was conscious and coherent. Hastings did everything he could to stem the bleeding. Fortunately carrying a park radio, he called park headquarters, relating the incident and the serious physical injuries.

Park Ranger Tom Black, a medical flight technician, immediately left Mammoth Hot Springs in a small helicopter with a pilot. They flew directly toward Bighorn Pass and located the site. They landed the copter in a small meadow some distance below the site. Black immediately tended to Barry Gilbert and realized the seriousness of his condition. He called for smoke jumpers out of West Yellowstone to carry Gilbert down off the mountain to a more suitable departure site.

Gilbert later attributed Black's efforts in stopping the persistent blood flow with saving his life. Gilbert was flown by helicopter to the Yellowstone Lake Hospital. After remedial care, he was airlifted to a Salt Lake City hospital. There was some in-house discussion in the National Park Service relative to precautions that should have been provided. The researchers had arrived only recently, and the area was new to them.

Therefore, possibly greater indoctrination or an experienced monitor might have avoided the scars that Barry Gilbert carries today.

Gilbert devoted his later studies to grizzly bears and brown bears in Alaska and Canada. His major direction in research has been on how to manage people and grizzly bears when large numbers of both come together.

The Gallatin Mountain Range in Yellowstone was favorable grizzly habitat and the least traveled by park visitors. Grizzly encounters were not frequent, and the bears were rightly disturbed by humans.

In 1945 I helped Ernie Miller of the Elkhorn Ranch pack onto Quadrant Mountain just north of Big Horn Pass about four airline miles from the Gilbert encounter. Assistant Chief Ranger Al Elliott was in charge, and I was tending the horses. This location was previously acknowledged to be an excellent area for photographing grizzly bears – preferably with a telephoto lens.

We rode out of Fawn Creek Patrol Cabin and on top of Quadrant Mountain. We spotted grizzly bears in two distant locations. We decided to try and approach a grizzly with two cubs. I tied up the horses in some small trees about one-quarter mile away from the mother bear.

Ernie Miller was using a 16mm movie camera and took some pictures at about 300 yards. As he and Al Elliott moved forward, I returned to the horses. I waited and waited, and then I heard a great amount of shouting. I ran forward and found a very dejected Ernie Miller. There were no bears in sight, but Miller and Elliott had just experienced a rather hair-raising experience. Evidently Miller kept moving his tripod and camera closer and closer, whereby Elliott reportedly told him, "Ernie Miller, you're going to get us into trouble."

Ernie had moved to within 100 yards of the grizzly when she spotted him and charged. Now this bear didn't come alone but her cubs came at her side. Elliott had moved away a bit and Ernie was fast trying to get away from his camera setup.

The grizzly charged the camera, knocking it over, bending the tripod all out of shape, and batting the camera. Ernie was trying to seek some cover but as he stated, "One of those damn cubs was trying to chew my legs off." When the cubs ran back to their mother, still at the camera, she decided to slowly leave.

We gathered up the twisted tripod and damaged camera. As Elliott finally stated, "This was the first time I ever witnessed a grizzly bear provoked enough to charge and nearly destroy a camera."

In 1957 Glacier National Park authorities requested that I interview a young photographer in the hospital in Kalispell, Montana, who had been severely mauled by a grizzly bear. This incident took place on Siyeh Creek, just east and down the mountain from Logan Pass and north of the Going-to-the-Sun Road. This poor fellow was a mess of bandages but feeling much better after four days in the hospital. His statement was: "I observed a grizzly bear in hiking up Siyeh Creek at a distance of about 300 yards and set up my camera with tripod and telephoto lens. From this observation I determined she had with her two, probably yearling, cubs. To get close I packed up my gear and contoured up the hillside, hiking to where I estimated I should be able to get better pictures. However, a low ridge obstructed my view. So on hands and knees I crawled up the ridge and the bears were now not over 50 yards away. Not using the tripod, I shot several pictures. Then I thought maybe I could stand up and use the tripod for more steady pictures. Well, the mother immediately charged me, knocked me down chewing my one leg, shoulder, and clawed my neck and face. Evidently the mother bear observed the yearlings leaving the scene and she rather reluctantly departed." I asked if he had any thoughts about why the incident occurred. He replied, "I guess I just got too close but didn't really expect her to attack me, rather thought she would scamper away."

For three seasons, 1946-48, I was assigned to a coyote migration study by the U.S. Fish and Wildlife Service out of their research laboratory at Denver, Colorado. This effort necessitated tagging and marking coyote pups at den sites in May and June, and trapping and marking adult coyotes in the fall. The study area was the northern section of Yellowstone National Park and southern Park and Gallatin counties in Montana. In three years more than 400 coyotes were tagged and marked to determine the seasonal drift of coyotes.

Starting in the third year of the study, marked coyotes were collected. Their cropped ears were highly visible, which prevented unmarked coyotes from being collected. Weldon Robinson, project leader, and I had been collecting marked coyotes in the northern part of Yellowstone by using animal distress calls to lure coyotes within shooting range.

In early 1948 a tagged and marked coyote was reported in Hayden Valley near lower Otter Creek. One early morning in late June we attempted to locate the marked coyote. We were both equipped with .270-caliber rifles, and we were traveling up a ridge between Otter Creek on our right and some open meadowland on our left. Our intention was to travel up the ridge to a more timbered section and initiate a distress call, hoping to call in the marked coyote. We were traveling through scattered mature lodgepole pines on the west side of the ridge crest so we could not be seen from the more open meadowland on the east side, where the coyote had been observed the previous day. I was in the lead with Robinson spaced a bit behind, and we were very silently proceeding up the ridge. Suddenly I could see the back of a grizzly bear just over the crest of the ridge less than 100 feet away. A split second later I observed the backs of two apparent yearlings. I assumed they were feeding on vegetation as I couldn't see their heads or legs, but I was certain it was a grizzly and cubs. I instantly dropped down on my hands and knees to sneak away from the bears, and I placed my index finger to my lips to indicate to Robinson, "no talk." He bent down low and came to my position, and we beat a hasty retreat downhill toward Otter Creek. Now we could hear the mother grizzly, huffing and puffing up on the ridge, but we did not see her again.

The following day I was a bit ill, so Robinson alone went back to Hayden Valley in an attempt to collect the marked coyote. Very early in the morning he was hiking up the same ridge and passed the site where I had observed the grizzly bears the previous day. After traveling farther on, he came into dense timber and immediately saw the female grizzly with two yearling cubs. The mother was on top of the ridge about 200 yards away. She had detected an undetermined movement and came toward Robinson in a fast walk. This was not a new venture for Robinson as in his many years with the Fish and Wildlife Service he had experienced similar situations. He was quite sure the mother grizzly came toward him thinking he was a deer or an elk calf.

Robinson was standing behind a large, dead, lodgepole pine

so perhaps the bear could not identify him. Robinson stepped out and started talking to her. The mother bear stopped momentarily, watching the human before her. Then she charged and Robinson fired a shot from his rifle into the ground. The bear hesitated but came forward again. As she reached the dead tree with Robinson behind it, she reared up and batted the tree with one of her paws, knocking rotten wood particles into Robinson's face. Again he fired into the ground and the mother bear reluctantly and slowly departed.

That evening back in Gardiner, Montana, Robinson stated, "I found out today why you hit the ground and crawled off that ridge yesterday." He had not seen the bears the day before so he had only my word of their being there. "At first I thought maybe you had fainted or had a heart attack, but today that old grizzly bear damn near gave me one. Plus, it sure wouldn't be very appropriate for a coyote researcher to shoot a grizzly bear inside Yellowstone National Park."

Unfortunately, in the early fall of 1986, William Lesinsky, a photographer from Great Falls, Montana, was killed at this same location. Lesinsky started up the same ridge, spotted a female grizzly with cubs in the upper end of the meadow, and apparently came down off the ridge on the east side. When attempting to photograph the bears, he was attacked, killed, and partly eaten. Being alone, his body was not discovered until his unattended vehicle prompted a search for him.

In late July 1984, a campfire permit was issued at Canyon Ranger Station in Yellowstone to a Brigitta Claudia Fredenhogen of Basel, Switzerland. This backcountry camping permit was for July 30 and 31 in the White Lake area north of Yellowstone Lake. This individual was cautioned that solitary hiking and camping in this area was discouraged due to the prevalence of grizzly bears. However, Brigitta had a considerable record of visiting remote wilderness-type areas both in the U.S. and Europe. By prearrangement, Brigitta was to meet her brother at the Canyon Ranger Station either late evening on July 31 or early on August 1. Due to her being overdue on August 1, Ranger Mark Marschall was dispatched to the campsite designated by her permit, located at a trail junction. He found no evidence of her camping there, so he followed an alternate trail toward Fern Lake Cabin. Finally at a numbered site at the outlet of White Lake, he found her pack frame and some belongings. Up the slope in the timber Marschall located her torn sleeping bag and, beyond that, her badly mutilated body, partly eaten.

This was a most disturbing ending for this well-qualified hiker, but safety in numbers, such as a hiking partner, may have reduced the opportunity for such an unfortunate event. Campsites that are adjacent to trail junctions should be relocated, preferably 200 yards or more off such trails. In the 1980s many Yellowstone backcountry campsites were moved close to trails and trail junctions for camper convenience and ease of accountability by the National Park Service. In areas of grizzly bear preferred habitat, managers are challenged to implement adjustments toward greater safety of backcountry visitors. There is hardly a day that fresh grizzly tracks cannot be observed on the dusty trails in these localities. From Pelican Cone Lookout I have observed grizzly bears, in the evening, traveling hiking trails to whatever destinations they had in mind.

FEEDING GROUNDS
AND DUMPS

IN the 1920s and 1930s, feeding grounds for bears became popular with Yellowstone visitors. At these places they could see both grizzly and black bears.

The first bear feeding ground was established in the 1920s at Old Faithful. It expanded to two elevated platforms and acquired the title "Bear Feeding Lecture Stadium." It eventually accommodated a seating capacity of nearly 3,000 visitors. Food was placed on the platforms to attract bears from the forest background. Front-row visitors were seated behind a taut, stretched cable about 100 feet from the bears. The 7 p.m. lecture was conducted by a ranger on horseback between the bears and the visiting public. Horses with considerable exposure to this activity expressed little fear of the bears in spite of the close quarters. Ranger Phillip Martindale was the lecturer for many years and stated it took nearly four years for the bears, both black and grizzly, to become accustomed to his voice and less timid about approaching the feeding platforms.

The Old Faithful "bear feeding stadium" gradually became a problem due to its intense popularity and large visitor audiences. Expansion of utility and visitor service accommodations at Old Faithful had encroached near the site, and threatening bear encounters were on the increase. Although the lecture program was well presented and received, covering various subjects on Yellowstone's wild animals, the unnatural condition was questioned. The program at Old Faithful was terminated in 1936.

At the Grand Canyon of the Yellowstone there had been several dumpsites throughout earlier years. These sites were near the Canyon Hotel on the west side of the Canyon and on the east side not too far from Canyon Lodge. Later all refuse was hauled to a central site off the Norris-Canyon road. In the early 1930s the Otter Creek Bear Feeding Ground was developed to afford park visitors a protected opportunity to view grizzly bears, accompanied by a lecture series. This project was planned with a vehicle parking area off the northeast side of a prominent ridge. Timbered steps about 12 feet wide, bordered on each side by a 7-foot cyclone fence, led to the summit of the ridge. Then the strong fence extended left and right down a grassy slope in a westerly direction and across the creek bottom in a near north-south direction. The fence enclosed a section just up the slope from the grassy bottomland of Otter Creek. Beyond this section to the west about 50 yards was the level feeding area, estimated at about 16 feet by 100 feet, which in later years was made a concrete pad. A water supply from a spring was piped down to the pad and enclosed within a concrete vault with a manhole cover for access. A fuel-oil hot water heater provided hot water for cleaning the feeding pad.

The west slope within the enclosure was designed with benches to seat about 1,500 visitors, and starting in 1938 two lectures a night were conducted. The bears were shielded from sight of the parking lot and the ridge was somewhat of a sound barrier. A ranger with a rifle was always stationed at the entrance to the enclosure in the parking lot. Thus, visitors were inside the enclosure and the bears were outside.

While attending college in Bozeman, Montana, from 1938 to 1941, I was employed by the National Park Service Sanitation Division at Fishing Bridge. On a few occasions in 1940 I was delegated to assist Henry Rahn at Canyon in putting out feed for the bears at Otter Creek. Edible material, some vegetables but mostly meat scraps, was put in separate garbage cans at the government mess hall, Canyon Hotel, Pryor's Store, and the Canyon Lodge. This material was deposited at the Canyon Incinerator and collected by park sanitation employees in late afternoon and usually deposited on the Otter Creek feeding pad that day.

Henry Rahn and Bill Hall had been doing this task for a number of years, and I immediately noticed their only weapon for defense was a long, hardwood mattock with the iron pick and blade cut off, leaving the wide metal collar around the lower end of the handle—truly a dependable weapon. Normally there would not be any bears on the pad as we put out the food. Sometimes a few bears would observe us from the timbered ridge to the west. There were, on occasion, a few bears that approached the pad before we finished our task. One time several grizzly bears came down to the pad and walked around the truck. One big guy decided to climb onto the truck by putting both paws on top of the 8-inch sideboards. Henry, with no words of alarm, quickly picked up the mattock and bashed the large bear on one of its paws. The bear's immediate rapid departure disbursed the other grizzlies and we continued our work without further incident.

Dr. Phillip Fix, the ranger lecturer at Canyon, was the biology teacher at Gallatin County High School in Bozeman,

These photos, taken in 1940, show the author, Bob Murphy (top photo) and Henry Rahn (bottom photo) cleaning the Otter Creek Bear Feeding Ground in Yellowstone. The men usually cleaned the feeding platform, a 14 x 70 foot concrete pad, early in the mornings when bears were not around. Water from a nearby spring was piped to the pad and heated with a fuel-oil heater so the pad could be washed off with soap and water.

Montana. He had lectured at the feeding ground for several years prior to its termination at the close of the 1941 season.

One evening in August 1940, as I had in the past, I visited with Dr. Fix and asked him how many grizzly bears he estimated came to the bear feeding ground. Without much hesitation he stated there were about 74 grizzlies that visited the feeding ground. Some came every night, others two or three times a week, and a few grizzlies came only sporadically each season. As we were visiting, a very large and very thin grizzly charged from the west ridge to the feeding pad. There was great turmoil as the group of grizzlies already at the pad scattered left and right from the approaching bear. Apparently getting scent of the human visitors present, this very large grizzly reared up on his hind legs and then departed in a hurry up the ridge to the west and into the woods, not to be seen again. Dr. Fix stated, "That's a grizzly I'd not seen before this season."

During that same season there was a very large female black bear with two very small black cubs that frequently came to the feeding ground. Black bears often came to the site early to feed but normally departed when the pad became crowded with grizzlies. But this mother black bear didn't take a back seat to any grizzly, and the more difficult the challenge, the more aggressive she became. In fact she would literally fly at her opponents, even the largest of grizzlies, and she usually controlled one section of the pad.

This mother black bear would park her two cubs up the slope west of the feeding pad and come down to eat. Being a very nervous mother, she would charge up the hill to gather her cubs whenever grizzlies came off the same slope. Invariably, after two or more dashes up the slope to protect her cubs, she would move them to the east between the visitor enclosure

Grizzly bears and black bears gathered by the dozens at the Otter Creek Bear Feeding Ground in 1940. These photos show the bears, mostly grizzlies, on the feeding pad as food is being disbursed from a truck (a corner of the truck is visible in the top photo). The bear-watching area had seating for 1,500 people and rangers gave nightly programs.

and the feeding pad. Generally grizzlies didn't venture very far off the pad toward the visitor location.

From this location the mother black bear appeared a little less attentive, and the cubs, as the season went on, would occasionally go down to her side on the pad. She would almost immediately chase them back toward the visitor enclosure.

One night in late August I took some eastern friends to the bear-feeding lecture. The mother black bear was there in the pit with her cubs parked toward the visitor enclosure. As we listened to Dr. Fix's lecture, more grizzlies came down the slope from the west. It seemed that every time the cubs saw grizzlies coming they would seek the protection of their mother on the pad. Time and again she would chase them back toward the visitor enclosure.

This activity had been repeated about three times when it appeared the mother black bear had met a very large, challenging grizzly. With her cubs at her side, she charged this unrelenting bear and an apparent second challenger. The first grizzly, no doubt a large male, smothered one of the black bear cubs with his front paw. The mother bear charged again and again but the male grizzly merely pivoted around on the foot that pinned the cub underneath it. There was much screaming by park visitors - many "Oh no's." All the commotion caused most of the bears to leave, including the mother black bear with her one remaining cub. As this was happening the male grizzly started eating the pinned cub, and horrified visitors screamed even more. The noise caused the grizzly to depart up the hillside to the west with the remains of the little cub in his mouth. To add to this unfavorable and sensitive situation, the grizzly stopped about half way up the slope, lay down, and proceeded to devour his prey. Eventually he continued into the timber with what remained of the cub.

Fortunately this incident was near the end of the lecture. Many visitors, especially young ones, were in tears as they departed. Dr. Fix did all he could to explain the ways of the grizzly and nature's ways. It wasn't an easy task to further explain the incident to my eastern friends.

As war clouds developed over Europe in 1941, park visitation decreased rapidly. Lodges, hotels, and many visitor service facilities were closed in late August. Fewer visitors meant less leftover food for the bears, so the Otter Creek Bear Feeding program was closed on August 21.

Sentiment against these unnatural feeding situations had been growing for some time. Additional wartime travel restrictions anticipated for 1942 and other circumstances afforded the National Park Service the opportunity to discontinue this attraction for all time. This removed one of the unnatural conditions which had grown in the park through popular demand.

In evaluating the ecology of bears in Yellowstone, many "spur of the moment" authors or slanted journalists extract segments of time in formulating conclusions about management. Only in recent years has in-depth research formulated guidance in this endeavor. Yet political influence, lacking basic principles of research, has exerted undue pressures in guiding management.

In earliest times during the military administration of the park, dumping grounds were established to dispose of refuse, both edible and non-edible material. This created locations where black and grizzly bears foraged for supplemental food.

Increased visitation in the 1920s and early 1930s created more refuse, and additional dumps were created. During this period there were dump grounds at every major visitor area plus road maintenance camps and contractor camps. Such locations attracted many bears and no doubt contributed to increased black bear populations.

Bituminous surfacing of park roads was started in the mid 1930s. A number of approach roads to Yellowstone National Park were not totally bituminous surfaced until the 1936-38 time period. As a result of these improved roads, park visitation rapidly increased, creating traffic problems including "bear jams" and additional bear-injury reports.

A factor of development that has not been addressed by most writers was the incinerators constructed at major locations in the park and their effects on bears searching for food.

An incinerator was constructed at Old Faithful in 1928 to dispose of all garbage, including edible waste, from the hotel, lodge, government mess, Hamilton Stores, and all operators in the area. In 1929 an incinerator was built at Yellowstone Lake between the Lodge Cabins and the government horse barn. In 1929-30 an incinerator was built at Canyon in a clearing southwest of Chittenden Bridge. In 1930-31 an incinerator was built at Mammoth Hot Springs below the present elementary school and at Fishing Bridge about three-fourths of a mile north of the ranger station. In 1932 an incinerator was constructed at West Thumb south of the development area. The incinerators during this period were fired by wood, mostly lodgepole pine cut into lengths of six to seven feet.

To dispose of materials that could not be accommodated at the incinerators, major dump grounds were concentrated at

Mammoth, Gardiner (within the park boundary), Fishing Bridge, Canyon, Thumb, and Old Faithful. Many discarded vehicles, wagons, and other large objects went to Mammoth Hot Springs. A dump ground at West Yellowstone, Montana, also attracted a number of grizzly bears.

With the use of the incinerators, many of the minor dump grounds were cleaned up and closed. The cessation of edible materials on dump grounds had a profound effect on bears, especially black bears. There was a noticeable increase in black bears at major campgrounds. Nightly visits by grizzly bears were not uncommon. The garbage containers at the time were more or less an open door for scavenger bears. Some were located on decks outside of hotels and lodges. In campgrounds, many garbage cans were located on elevated structures for ease in transporting the cans to flatbed garbage trucks. Sometimes black bears would perch upon these structures, preventing the more timid park visitors from depositing their garbage.

Bear-proof garbage can covers were widely installed at all major campgrounds between 1965 and 1969. This had a profound effect on reducing forage available in campgrounds, especially for black bears, likely stimulating a wide dispersal for mere survival. In subsequent years the number of black bears in campgrounds was drastically reduced, due mainly to diminished food supply.

The transition from wood-fired incinerators to oil-fired incinerators was undertaken in the late 1960s. This was deemed necessary due to the age of the wood-fired units, more efficient and rapid incineration with the newer incinerators, and less pollution. New locations for oil-burning incinerators were limited to Bridge Bay (Weasel Creek), Grant Village (to the southwest), Mammoth Hot Springs (near the site of the old incinerator), and at Madison Junction (west of the campground).

The combination of variables that affected supplemental forage for bears extended over many years, with ups and downs—no doubt confusing to the bears.

Since 1970 all garbage has been removed from Yellowstone National Park, Cooke City, and Silver Gate, Montana, and trucked to disposal centers at West Yellowstone and Livingston, Montana. This action, plus former efforts in reducing available supplemental forage, has resulted in a wide dispersal of bears into natural foraging areas, thus reducing bear observations by visitors around campgrounds and other developed visitor sites.

EMBARRASSING SITUATIONS

THERE was a young black bear that frequented West Thumb Campground in 1954. It was probably two years old and somewhat timid but persisted in being a daytime visitor to the campground.

In 1955 this bear was again a constant visitor and exhibited a more brazen approach to visitors. He had also graduated to breaking into the camping properties of park visitors. The rangers live-trapped the bear twice during the summer and released him into remote, uninhabited areas of the park. Each time he found his way back to the Thumb area.

In late summer the bear started following visitors to the garbage cans so he could immediately inspect what they had deposited. Then he'd dominate the scene and would not let other people approach and deposit their garbage. Then this bear evidently decided there was a more direct way to get food.

One day a lady campground visitor exited her trailer and headed for the garbage cans enclosed in an elevated deck. This bear charged her and she either dropped the garbage or the bear took it from her. She was so frightened, the lady wasn't positive whether the bear knocked her down or she fell trying to escape the bear. In any case, the bear escaped with whatever goodies the parcel contained and the lady ruined a good pair of stockings and received two bloody knees and a really bruised elbow.

The information was relayed to me at Lake Ranger Station, and I was urged to come to West Thumb and deal with the problem. It was early evening. I picked up a rifle and my wife wanted to go along—mistake number one! We headed for West Thumb Ranger Station where I conversed with a couple of seasonal rangers. They were both really "shook" over the conduct of this bear and really didn't want to see him destroyed. He was a beautiful, black, shiny bear with a white V on his chest. About this time I was thinking, with all this sentiment, maybe I should just go back to Lake. I did go talk to the lady who had been injured, and she too had sympathy for the bear but really believed he was a danger to people in the campground.

So I parked the pickup and, with my rifle, started a walk around the wooded area outside the campground. Finally I came upon the bear. He wasn't afraid of me but exhibited no aggression; he was a smooth operator. I walked toward him and he decided to escape my aggression by climbing a large tree that had a fork near the top. This wise guy crawled into the fork and looked down at me.

Again I was thinking, I should just go back to Lake, but I looked around and here came my wife, the injured lady, and about eight curious souls. So I had to get this thing over with. I aimed between the bear's eyes and pulled the trigger. Well, he dropped his head and blood streamed down the side of the tree and onto the ground. The bear slumped into the crotch of the tree and was obviously going to stay there.

So I hung my damned head and went back to the ranger station, got a pair of leg tree climbers, and came back to the scene. I climbed the tree and kicked the bear out of the fork in the tree and down to the ground—he was very dead. I dreaded such unfortunate results and headed back to Lake Ranger Station thinking this was not the most rewarding occupation.

In September 1939 I was confined to the Mammoth Hot Springs Hospital with a couple of fractures to the fingers of my left hand. My roommate became Park Ranger Leon Evans who was also recuperating from surgery. Leon soon became an Assistant Chief Ranger at Yellowstone National Park and later the Superintendent of National Parks in the southwest.

During our short stay in the hospital, we shared many experiences concerning park visitors, law enforcement, forest fires, and wildlife. Some of the most interesting experiences concerned the bears of Yellowstone. One story that has remained in my memory was the one Evans experienced at Old Faithful Inn with an averaged-sized black bear in 1937.

A telephone call was received at the Old Faithful Ranger Station about 6 a.m. from Tex Hammond, the night watchman at the inn, that a bear was inside the inn's lobby. He and the cook's assistant had no luck chasing the bear out of the lobby.

The subsequent article in the *Salt Lake Tribune*, dated Sunday morning, August 22, 1937, was interesting yet only a bit in error:

Hospitable Old Faithful Inn Turns Away Grizzly Guest

Yellowstone, Wyo. Aug 21. – The usually hospitable Old Faithful Inn was forced to turn away a guest on Saturday. Just as the sun was breaking over the eastern hills, a 250-pound black bear padded up to the hotel desk. Tex Hammond, night watchman, peered through the dim light and decided bears aren't welcome.

Tex strode out from behind the desk and made motions to the uninvited guest to scram. The bear lumbered and floundered over couches, divans, chairs and tables with Tex at his heels.

After a few minutes the bear tired of being "it" in that particular game of tag.

Bruin wheeled on Tex and Tex wheeled.

Off they went in the opposite direction, with Tex leading by a whisper. Tex leaped over a table that the bear could not negotiate and increased his margin enough to get to a telephone booth. Here he put in a hurried call for a ranger with sharp eyes, a rifle and a deadly aim.

Meanwhile the bear, on his first visit to the Inn, began to inspect the accommodations. He had climbed up through the open court lobby to the fourth floor when Ranger Leon Evans arrived on the scene. Evans drew a bead, fired once, and the bear dropped 40 feet to the lobby floor, a bullet between his eyes.

The actual story went like this: Ranger Evans left his quarters at the Old Faithful Ranger Station shortly after the call from Hammond. He took along a .270-caliber rifle and drove to the back door of the inn. There he was met by a really excited cook and his assistant. The assistant explained that he had earlier cleaned and mopped the kitchen floor and opened the back door to expedite the drying of the floor. He then went out of the kitchen momentarily and upon returning observed a bear. He grabbed a broom and attempted to chase the bear out the open door. Instead, the bear ran through the open entry into the lobby of the inn. The assistant to the cook hollered to the night watchman, "There's a bear in the lobby," and closed the entry to the kitchen. The lobby was a huge, cavernous expanse of intricately designed log structures extending three stories in height. The bear climbed up to one of the horizontal log beams and there it rested, peering down at the frustrated night watchman.

When Ranger Evans entered the lobby, he attempted to talk the bear down from its perched location. His efforts caused the bear to climb higher. The cook then pressed the ranger to do something soon because in a few minutes guests would be coming to breakfast into the adjacent dining room. The only quick solution was to dispatch the bear, whereupon Evans shot it. The rifle blast echoed throughout the inn and the bear tumbled down with a bang onto the lobby floor.

As the bear was very dead, Evans immediately secured a rope and dragged the bear out the back door of the kitchen and onto the bed of his truck. The cook and his assistant feverishly mopped blood from the floor.

Evans briefly discussed the situation with the inn attendants and checked the kitchen for any damage the bear might have caused. He noticed a few guests arriving for breakfast. Evans said, "If those guests had known about the foregoing event of that bear high up in the lobby, I'm sure they would have been a little more nervous."

PAINFUL AND HUMOROUS

AT times, ranger contacts with park visitors who have had close encounters with bears may be frustrating to the officer and entail painful sessions. At other times an incident may produce a degree of usually suppressed humor.

On a rainy afternoon while driving a patrol car from Norris Junction to Mammoth Hot Springs, I encountered a bear-automobile incident. Far down a straight stretch of the wet road I saw a large black bear standing against a parked car. As I slowly approached in my car, I saw the male driver feeding marshmallows to the bear through the driver's window. The female passenger, also in the front seat, was exhibiting considerable fear as the male driver held marshmallows inside the car toward her and the bear stuck its head deep into the car's interior to snap up the delicacies.

I stopped behind the vehicle with the patrol car's red light turned on, indicating a warning for feeding the bear. The driver immediately started his vehicle and moved it slowly forward, but the bear's paws were still resting on the opening of the car window. It was odd to observe the bear sidestepping one foot over the other to keep up with the slowly moving vehicle. Then the driver rolled up the window until the bear's paws were viced between the glass and the top of the door. The driver stopped the car and rolled down the glass a bit, evidently believing the bear would remove his paws. No such luck! The driver started the car forward again, rolling up the window with the bear sidestepping down the road with its paws caught in the top of the window.

It was evident to me that this bear was not going to play this game much longer. Suddenly the bear reared back and yanked the window from the door, shattering the glass on the asphalt road. I turned on the siren to pull over the driver. He was most apologetic and his wife was obviously relating an, "I told you it was a dumb act and I was really frightened - you deserve to be arrested." I gave the driver a warning and told him to clean up the glass. The damage was likely a bit costly. I saw the bear in the woods, peering back at the scene, and I thought I detected a slight smile on its face.

***

One time, driving west from Tower Falls, I saw an elderly couple standing off the road, feeding a black bear and two cubs. The elderly gentleman took several pictures of his companion, probably his wife, feeding marshmallows to the mother bear and separately feeding the cubs. The photographer then took a real close-up of the mother bear as she stood on her hind legs facing him. His wife left for their automobile. The photographer then turned his back toward the bear and held up his camera at eye level, advancing the film. This mother bear obviously wanted some additional marshmallows and moved to the photographer. With a swift swat with one of her front paws to the man's posterior, she completely removed the seat of his pants and blood flowed from his right hip.

I told the gentleman that there was not an excessive amount of sympathy for his misfortune but I bandaged his leg and instructed him to check in with the nurse at Mammoth Hot Springs.

***

One evening at Lake Ranger Station, a Japanese gentleman rushed into the office with his 16-year-old daughter. She had been injured by a small black bear at the Fishing Bridge cabins where they were staying.

The daughter was in considerable pain and blood flowed from puncture wounds on the calf of her right leg. The bear had bitten into both the inside and outside of the muscle and one puncture exhibited a tearing wound. She was bandaged and a ranger transported her to the nurse's office at Lake Hotel for further attention and likely a tetanus shot.

The father was questioned as to how the accident happened. He stated, "A small bear had tipped over a garbage can next to their cabin. He coaxed his 12-year-old daughter to stand by the bear, which had its head and half its body inside the garbage can, for a picture." The bear remained occupied in its feeding and exhibited no concern. The father then asked his 16-year-old daughter to straddle the small bear for a picture. Just as she was positioned over the bear, the animal backed out of the garbage can. Evidently the bear recognized it was in close quarters with a human and, no doubt frightened, bit the girl's leg and then scampered away.

An effort was made to impress the gentleman that bears were wild animals and that close encounters were frequently painful and many times disastrous.

IT WAS BEST TO BE ON HORSEBACK

TWICE I was assigned to the Thorofare Ranger Station to patrol the area during the fall hunting seasons outside the park. These assignments also entailed cabin maintenance, taking rations to various patrol cabins, and packing in hay and oats for the horses and mules.

In late September 1943, I was traveling on horseback and leading four pack mules on the trail along the east shore of Yellowstone Lake. There was about four inches of fresh snow. After leaving Clear Creek heading south, I noticed the tracks of a large grizzly bear on the trail. The tracks stayed on the trail for about a mile. Later the tracks came back onto the trail but disappeared before Park Point Patrol Cabin.

After leaving rations at the cabin for the winter ski patrols and splitting some wood, I continued south. After about two miles, the grizzly bear tracks were noted again in the trail, also headed south. I was riding through a rather dense lodgepole forest approaching Columbine Creek. Suddenly a grizzly bear exploded out of the timber to my right. He crossed the trail and headed into a mess of downed timber and was obviously having difficulty trying to escape. Apparently when we approached the bear had been busy tearing into an old rotten log on the side of the trail.

Seeing the bear, the mules moved forward in a very curious and alert attitude. One mule came up beside me on the right, one on my left, and the lead rope between the mules became stretched over the back of my saddle horse and hung up under the cantle of my saddle. The grizzly bear became frustrated with his lack of progress over and under the timber downfall. He turned around and headed back toward the trail, and he was moaning and the hairs over his back were bristled out and he was very unhappy. He would have intercepted the trail not more than 100 feet below us. Well, one mule let out a bray and then they all tried to turn back down the trail. We became so entangled that no one, horses, mules or yours truly, could go anywhere. The bear came back to the trail and turned south, really streaking away from us. After a degree of profanity I finally untangled the wreck and headed on down the trail toward Thorofare.

Later that fall, Jack Hoppe, who had been working on trail maintenance with four additional pack mules, came to the Trail Creek Cabin. This location was on the south end of the Southeast Arm of Yellowstone Lake. On the boat dock others had stacked wire-tied baled hay. Jack and I made two trips packing the hay up the Yellowstone River to the Thorofare Ranger Station and storing the bales in the barn.

We had rations for Fox Creek Cabin over on the headwaters of the Snake River, plus other supplies and two new mattresses. As Jack was occupied in repairing the Trail Creek corral, I took off with four mules for Fox Creek, traveling up Chipmunk Creek and onto Two Ocean Plateau. On the plateau there was a real blizzard with large snowflakes coming down.

It was a wide-open, sub-alpine country with grass and sedges and an occasional small clump of alpine fir. In approaching one of these alpine clusters I could barely see an animal off to my right a little less than 200 yards away. As we drew closer I suddenly became aware it was a grizzly, busy digging into the turf. The mules and my saddle horse didn't seem to pay any attention, maybe because the bear was nearly motionless. The bear suddenly discontinued his ground search, turned sideways, and just stared at us in a frozen position. We never stopped but kept going down the trail, and he still stared at us. When I again looked back, the bear had resumed its digging. Maybe he just thought we were some elk because the wind was wrong for him to smell us.

CHASING SMOKE

DURING the summer of 1943 many employees of the National Park Service at Yellowstone went off to World War II, and others thought they might be called to duty. Manpower for fighting forest fires was in short supply, especially in remote areas, due to the limited number of smokejumpers and aircraft available from the U.S. Forest Service. Several employees in Yellowstone hiked many miles into the backcountry to suppress lightning-ignited fires that season.

One day in late August, both Mt. Washburn and Pelican Cone lookouts reported a small fire just northwest of White Lake. I was designated to go into the area and attempt to put out the fire. In the event the fire was beyond my control, I was to call for reinforcements by radio.

The trip into Pelican Creek was uneventful, and I was able to drive the pickup to an old forest-fire base camp. I unloaded my gear: a Pulaski, a lady shovel, and a heavy backpack. The heaviest thing in the pack was the very cumbersome radio - it seemed to weigh a ton. I also had some C-rations, a first aid kit, a heavy jacket, and a 2.5-pound down sleeping bag.

I hiked up Astringent Creek to the divide and over into White Lake drainage, crossed Broad Creek at the outlet of the lake, then hiked along its northeast shore through the lodgepole forest to a big grassland park where there were a number of hot springs. The location was called "Ponuntpa Springs." From this location I saw smoke in a small canyon to the northwest.

The sun had disappeared over the western horizon and the light was growing dim. I started hiking across the large grassland and was less than half way across when I spotted an animal, maybe a buffalo, just ahead of me and slightly to my left. Shortly I became aware it was a large grizzly occupied in digging up whatever was below ground level.

I immediately backtracked to the forest and circled around to my right. This slowed my approach because it was more difficult traveling through the timber. I eventually arrived at the mouth of the small canyon, dropped my pack against a tree next to a very small stream, and continued to the fire. I removed some burnable fuel near the small blaze and then returned to the stream and my pack. That fire wasn't going anywhere and would still be a one-man fire in the morning. In the dark I ate my C-rations and wondered what direction that grizzly would depart Ponuntpa Springs. Would he come up this game trail that extended up the canyon?

I hung the pack in a tree and planned to call on the radio in the morning. I took a ground cloth and my sleeping bag about 150 yards off the game trail, pushed into a thicket of small lodgepole pines, and laid out my sleeping bag. I had my Pulaski, shovel, and a Forest Service-type flashlight with a metal battery box and a cord leading to a headlight. I placed the flashlight close to my sleeping bag. I was inside the bag, lying on my back and prepared to go to sleep. I couldn't get the damned grizzly off my mind. I don't know exactly how long I'd been asleep but I was suddenly awakened when something thumped me right in the stomach, and I thought "bear." I grasped for the flashlight and finally turned it on. I scanned the perimeter of the trees and listened, but I didn't hear or see anything.

Then off to my left I saw two snowshoe rabbits, probably the real culprits. I didn't really sleep too well the remainder of the night, sort of expecting some other intruder, maybe the bear. I put out the fire and departed the area the next afternoon. I have relived this episode many times—thankful the grizzly bear didn't come through my campsite.

IN DIM LIGHT

IN the summer of 1955 the rangers at West Thumb Ranger Station had considerable problems with a very large, brown, male black bear. This old bear had no fear of humans and was making a career of tearing into those little tear-drop trailers, the kind you unlatch the back end, prop it open, and do your cooking where a gas stove and groceries were stored. This bear could also steal groceries out of a tent without going through the entrance, either by crawling or reaching underneath the tent or by making a nice big hole in the side.

This brown black bear had been trapped on two occasions. Once hauled down toward the South Entrance below Lewis Lake, he was back at the West Thumb Campground in two days. The second time he was transported over the Continental Divide toward Old Faithful. Five days later he was back.

One evening at Lake Ranger Station I received a call from Duane Miller, Senior Seasonal Ranger at West Thumb, that this old bear was back, raising hell, and that we'd have to take other measures to cope with the problem. I knew it would be dark before I could get there, so I picked up a battery pack with a powerful spotlight plus a scoped 30-06 rifle.

At West Thumb Ranger Station there were three seasonal rangers in the office. We discussed alternatives in dealing with the bear. One suggested trapping him again and hauling the bear to Hayden Valley north of Fishing Bridge. Consensus was that we would just be transferring the problem to another locality. I finally stated, "This bear has been extended the opportunity to alter his foraging habits, and his living time has been, therefore, considerably diminished."

I asked for a volunteer and one seasonal ranger was "chomping at the bit" to go along. Juan Pardeau was a friendly fellow from way down in Texas and was of Spanish origin. He was a teacher during the school year, and I realized at the outset his bear experience was limited to the most casual observations.

We drove around several campground loops before we spotted this big brown bear near a trailer. I drove to a vacant parking area and told Juan, "We're going to walk this guy out of the campground into the woods and away from all these people." He immediately said, "What do you mean, walk him out?" I said, "We will just go over where he is, get behind him, and tag along. You have to take it easy, stay back and don't crowd him, and just hopefully worry him to the outside."

I gave Juan the battery pack that had the powerful spotlight. I had him practice pointing the light at an object and turning it on. "OK, let's go, but don't turn on that damned light until I tell you."

We walked the campground road about 200 yards and spotted the bear near a garbage can. We circled around to a location about 150 feet behind the bear with the forest out beyond him. The bear moved onto the campground road and I told Juan, "I think we've got it made." Well, this old bear had other ideas. He went up the road about 200 feet and then headed back toward the center of the campground. So we backtracked and got behind the bear again and got him heading in the right direction. This old bear went out to the edge of the campground and again turned back into the campground.

Now the bear knew we were shadowing him and he was not happy, grumbling and clicking his teeth. I was suspecting this old guy might be too smart to fall for our ploy.

The night sky was covered with broken clouds with a nearly full moon shining through at short intervals. Sometimes it was pretty dark and sometimes bright moonbeams streaked down onto the landscape. We tried one more time. We got behind the bear and were hazing him out of the campground. I was bothered because the bear kept looking back at us. We lost him between some tents and a couple of trailers, so we stopped. I told Juan, "Let's wait him out." After a short stop, I moved around one of the trailers and there he was not 25 feet away. The bear bolted into the forest.

We tagged along and fortunately the bear moved farther away from the campground. We came close to him again and he took off deeper into the forest. Again we came upon him, and I sensed he was growing tired of this game. He wasn't too eager to move again. This was likely the end of the road for him, and he just stood there.

I positioned Juan close behind me but slightly to my right. The bear was facing us. I braced against a tree and aimed the scoped rifle toward the bear about 75-80 feet away. I whispered, "Light." It came on, and when the light hit that bear, he charged straight at us. The light immediately went out and I heard footsteps rapidly leaving the area!

I hugged that damned tree and couldn't see a thing. I suspected the bear couldn't see too well either after the effects of the light. I heard the bear moaning a bit and suspected he was trying to locate me. Suddenly a moonbeam shined through the trees and I saw the bear about 40-50 feet away. He was facing me with his muzzle near the ground, moving his head from side to side, evidently trying to determine my exact location. With improved light from the moon, I saw the back of his neck. Quickly I pulled the trigger and the poor old bear had seen his last tear-drop trailer.

I was looking over the bear when Juan came back. He apologized all over the place and said, "When that bear charged, I just thought we had better get the hell out of here." I was about to chew out this guy clear down to his bones, but thought what the hell! "Juan you bastard, you leave me in the wood to wrestle with this bear and I can't see a damn thing because of the effects of that spotlight." We laughed and he commented, "Yes, but you had the rifle."

Back at the ranger station when I told the other rangers of the light going out, his buddies were really on his back. I'm sure Juan carried the embarrassment of his bear hunt for the remainder of the season.

A GRIZZLY BEAR IN A CABIN

IT was usually pretty quiet in mid-afternoon around the Fishing Bridge Cabin area. This balmy day in late August of 1944 was no exception; people were likely touring around the park or fishing on Yellowstone Lake.

At Lake Ranger Station it was the same, pretty quiet. It was a beautiful, cloudless day and I noticed, looking across the lake through the window from my desk, no apparent problems for boaters as there were only small waves lapping the sandy shore. The phone rang and I answered it, whereby Carl Glass, the manager of the Fishing Bridge Cabins, very calmly related, "Murph, we have a bear in a cabin and I think it's a grizzly. The occupants were gone fishing, probably out on the lake."

I asked, "How in the hell did he get into the cabin?" Carl laughed, "He chewed a hole in the corner of the cabin and crawled in. You know this cabin was constructed with lapped siding boards with framing posts on the outside, guess he just found a knot or defect and just chewed and clawed it into a large hole." Carl had gone over there with a key and unlocked the door and opened it slightly, but the grizzly just bluffed him out so he locked the door and left the bear inside. "Come by and I'll give you the key."

It crossed my mind that old Carl was being pretty accommodating, offering me a key to go into a cabin where a grizzly had taken up residence and wrestle him out of there. Anyhow, I arrived at the cabin office, and as Carl was busy with some customers, I picked up the key and cabin number and drove there and parked my pickup nearby.

The door of the cabin was solid wood without a glass to peek through, so with rifle in hand I went around back, viewing the splintered hole. This bear had really made quite an entry. There were pieces of boards lying all around and the hole was obviously large enough to accommodate a blind large hog. I peeked into the entry and saw the rear end of the grizzly, which was prone and busily eating some goodies on the floor. He didn't move. The place was a mess, the table tipped over on its side and whatever was on top of it all over the floor.

I thought, "This shouldn't be too difficult. I'll go back to the front door, unlock it, and bluff this guy out through the hole he made in the side of the cabin." First I opened a screen door that kind of hung up on the bottom threshold. Then I unlocked the main wooden door, and with my left hand on the doorknob, started moving the door in and out to scare this guy out of the cabin. He was busy eating the morsels on the floor and growled but didn't retreat. I held the door slightly open to survey the mess. Broken eggs, bacon wrappers, bread wrappers, a jelly jar, and much more littered the floor. I resumed waving the door in and out, whereupon the bear rose to his feet and charged toward the door, stopping just short of colliding with it. I again started waving the door in and out, stomped my feet, and in a commanding low voice (I didn't want to attract a human audience), urged the bear to exit the cabin through the hole in the wall. Instead this guy retreated to the far side of the cabin and appeared to ignore me. The grizzly was likely a three-year-old or more, as he appeared to be more mature than a two-year-old. At last I was more demanding with a few choice cuss words, whereupon he charged the door and swatted it with one of his paws. I immediately closed the door and reconsidered my efforts.

After a moment I propped open the screen door with a wooden stake and slowly opened the main door. Then I went around to the rear of the cabin and picked up a splintered piece of wooden siding. I knelt down next to the bear's entry hole and began banging the board on the floor of the cabin, hoping the bear would go out the open front door. Instead the bear retreated again to the dark corner of the cabin, feeding on an item in his possession. Back at the front door, I cautiously closed it. I was in somewhat of a quandary whether to leave the bear in the cabin, but I knew if the guests came back unannounced, someone could get seriously injured by this foraging bear.

Away from the cabin I saw two men watching my activity, probably thinking I was an escapee from a loony farm. I walked over to them and related the situation. They had a rather rural appearance, one in bib overalls and one in overalls. The one in overalls said, "I told Bert you must have something cornered in that cabin but never dreamt it was a bear." One of the gentlemen's wives showed up and said, "Oh no! Not a bear," and left immediately. I didn't need an audience, so I asked if they would be willing to post themselves up and down the entry road to keep people away. Then I went into the woods to find a long pole. When I returned, Louie Haker, driving the garbage truck, stopped and I told him of the situation and asked that he stop by a little later as I might need some help.

With the pole, about 14 feet long and about 4 inches in diameter at the base and 1.5 inches at the top, I returned to the cabin. I related my plan to the two guarding gentlemen, propped the screen door open with a stick, gently opened the main door, and departed quickly to the rear of the cabin. I pushed the pole through the hole in the wall. The bear was lying on the floor facing away from me. I jabbed the pole into the bear's hind quarter and quick as a flash the bear turned and grabbed the end of the pole in his mouth and shortened it about 10 inches. I continued this effort until the bear had shortened the pole so much that I couldn't reach him anymore. I gave up and knew I needed some alternate plan.

I regrouped with my two volunteer gentlemen and decided to try the front-door approach again. With rifle in hand, I started moving the inside door in and out. The grizzly moved toward the hole in the wall, and I thought maybe he was going to exit the cabin. I quit my harassment and waited, hoping the bear would leave. Well, this guy changed his mind and started toward the food remaining on the floor. I stepped into the cabin, trying to bluff him to the outside. Suddenly this guy was mad, clicking his teeth, drooling, and he charged me with his nose near the floor and the length of his neck exposed. Immediately I was in high gear retreating backward and, in doing so, fired a bullet into his neck, which unfortunately ended his career.

The most amazing thing, unknown to me, was that the screen door had closed behind me, and so in backing up, I plowed right through it, taking the screen and center panel with me. I was standing outside looking inside, watching the dying bear, before I realized my back hurt like hell as a result of breaking through that screen door.

By now there was quite an audience. Luckily Haker arrived with the garbage truck. We surveyed the bear and the conditions in the cabin, now with the bear's blood added to the mess of food items on the floor. With a rope we pulled the grizzly from the cabin and, using some planks for a ramp, skidded him onto the bed of the truck. About this time we had more volunteers than needed, so Haker pulled out for the nearest incinerator about a mile away.

I had just locked the door when the housekeeping team, a man and his wife, showed up. I told them they sure had a cleaning job and I didn't envy their task. In talking to them, some dude in a black tie and sport coat put his hand on my shoulder and inquired as to why I'd shot the bear. We others grinned, and after some hesitation I told the guy I really didn't know, but in some stretch of the imagination it was rather accidental.

After the closing of the Canyon Bear Feeding Ground in 1941 and the Trout Creek Dump Ground in subsequent years, bear problems continued. This was especially true with young grizzlies that were dependent on such sources for a partial food supply. There was always a feeling of sadness in having to dispose of a grizzly bear in such situations, but more recent trends to natural foraging have resulted in a reduction in such incidents.

HUNTING FOR A SPECIAL BEAR, JUNE 1943

ON occasion from the 1920s to 1940s, park rangers were called upon to collect wildlife specimens for various museums, mostly for the larger cities in the United States. Such museum officials usually arrived with a collection permit signed by the Secretary of the Interior.

On this particular occasion, the persons arriving were from the Los Angeles County Museum at Exposition Park. We were introduced to Mel Lincoln, the curator, and W. Beck, taxidermist, at the Lake Ranger Station. Both had traveled extensively in collecting specimens, including trips to Canada and Alaska. Their interest in Yellowstone was to secure a male and female grizzly for mounting and display in their museum.

Assistant Chief Ranger Leon Evans and Lake District Ranger DeLyle Stevens spent two days in Hayden Valley and collected a female grizzly which both Lincoln and Beck processed for shipment in a building not far from the ranger station.

Late on Friday afternoon Lincoln and Beck were in a position to accommodate another bear. Evans and Stevens had Saturdays and Sundays off, so Stevens assigned me to go to Pelican Valley to search for a large male grizzly. "Maybe you can possibly locate a bear even though you don't collect it," he said. Lincoln instructed me not to shoot the grizzly in the

61

head as the complete skeleton was to be given to the University of California. He gave me the telephone number for a motel in West Yellowstone where they were staying. He further emphasized they needed to process the bear as soon as possible after it was killed.

I was given a Winchester 30-06 bolt-action rifle with a peep sight and a box of 180-grain, bronze-point cartridges. I had sighted-in the gun previously and felt reasonably confident of its accuracy. I departed in a government pickup, traveled east of Fishing Bridge, turned left at Squaw Lake onto the fire road, and crossed Pelican Creek Bridge into Pelican Valley. I continued on the fire road, crossing Astringent Creek and again to Pelican Creek near the trailhead for Pelican Cone Lookout. Here I parked and hiked a little more than two miles to Pelican Creek Patrol Cabin.

I cleaned up the cabin a bit, fetched some water, and proceeded to cook dinner. As the sun was low in the sky, I decided to take my binoculars and rifle and hike down the stream to a high point about a mile away. I hadn't been on the point more than 15 minutes when I spotted, with my naked eye, what I thought was a buffalo emerging from the forest across the open valley. When I looked through binoculars, I muttered, "Christ! That's a bear and he's heading for Pelican Creek."

The bear was nearly a mile away and I knew I would have to go downstream nearly the same distance to intercept him. This was an open valley with grasslands and sagebrush in the drier regions and heavy, dense, slough grass in the creek bottoms. I found myself trotting down a trail for a little more than a half mile, passed the Pelican Creek Bridge, and into the creek bottom. It was not easy going but I had to keep a low profile to avoid detection by the grizzly bear. I arrived at a location that I thought should be reasonably close for intercepting the bear. I rested a few minutes and climbed up a low ridge to look around. I was hoping to catch up with the bear before he crossed the creek, but I didn't. Back down on the creek bottom I hiked another quarter mile and climbed a ridge to my left. I was busy glassing the terrain north of the creek when I noticed an object on my side of the creek and downstream about 300 yards. My binoculars revealed a really large grizzly, probably a male. He was busy digging up the turf, so I sat down and broke off the top of a sagebrush to rest my rifle on. He finally turned broadside but he was too far away. I knew I needed to cut the distance in half.

I went back down on the creek and followed it downstream about 150 yards, then traveled up a left-hand draw and crawled up a small ridge. The grizzly was still in the same place, digging, with its tail to me. I again broke off the top of a sagebrush and rested the forepart of the rifle over it. Now I was thinking, "This better be good because there are no trees within 400 yards and most of them are small second-growth lodgepole pines and there is little chance of climbing one."

I waited and watched this grizzly and his digging activities for about five minutes, and he finally turned broadside about 150 yards away. I very carefully aimed just off his left elbow and squeezed the trigger. At the report of the rifle the bear went down on his side with all four feet sticking out at a 45-degree angle. I extracted the empty cartridge and chambered a fresh one. The empty dropped in the grass near my legs and I picked it up. When I looked back at the bear, he was heading straight toward me. I was quite sure he was trying to escape the scene and didn't know where I was. I was immediately aiming with my sights on his chest. He was jumping over sagebrush and made a difficult target. Fortunately there was an open grassy spot about 80 yards from me that he would cross. As he entered this spot I was squeezing the trigger, but he fell from my sight picture. He was down flat, then he got up and turned to his right. He was squirting blood about two feet from his side. He was going away so I flattened out, sort of digging my own hole, and watched him. Finally I saw him traveling slowly about 150 yards to the west. I waited about three or four minutes and walked to where I last saw him. There was still plenty of blood. I looked to the southwest and saw the grizzly about 300 yards away, slowly heading toward a thick grove of small lodgepole pines. I slowly proceeded that way and sat down about 50 yards from the trees.

I didn't trust my timing so I waited 10 minutes by my watch. Then I started into the thicket, taking one step and listening, another step and listening. I was having some second thoughts: "Am I really this brave? Maybe I should come back in the morning, but what will I tell Mr. Lincoln?" Finally I spotted the back of the grizzly and my rifle was ready. I thought he was half standing up, and I waited and waited—no movement. I cautiously approached and discovered he was totally expired, but in dying he had pushed up and onto two small pines that held him off the ground. He was really, in my estimation, a very large grizzly and, lucky for me, a male. I peeled off my undershirt and tied it to a nearby tree, hoping my scent would ward off other bears and keep them from damaging this to-be-mounted specimen.

It was going to be totally dark in about 15 minutes, so I headed for the Pelican Creek Bridge about one mile to the east. There was no trail and I had to meander through swampy sedge grasses, sagebrush, and cinquefoil. I was preoccupied in a desire to reach the bridge by dark. I finally stumbled onto the faint fire road and crossed the bridge. It was still about three miles to my pickup and very dark. I had no flashlight. The Big Dipper and the North Star off to my left were the only illumination and very faint. I wondered if the bear I killed might have a vengeful relative coming to his funeral! More seriously, I knew that when bears were traveling and going to some predetermined destination, they often followed trails like the faint path I was following.

I finally reached Astringent Creek where a family of coyotes joined in a chorus of yipping and howling that was a little

Author Bob Murphy with the huge grizzly he collected for a museum display in 1943. The Yellowstone bear was estimated to weigh more than 800 pounds.

exciting and a bit unnerving. Suddenly, closer up Astringent Creek, another group of coyotes added to the vocal chorus and then just as suddenly grew silent. As I passed some large trees, an owl called out with some echoing hoots. I was therefore a bit edgy, and especially upon leaving Astringent Creek, I was off the fire road on a fainter track. Finally I reached my pickup, a welcome sight. I headed for Lake Ranger Station with thankfully bright headlights.

Back at Lake Ranger Station, I called District Ranger Stevens and related the news, a male grizzly. His response was, "What size?" I told him I thought it was a very large bear. He replied, "Hell, Murphy, they all look big!" Stevens called Lincoln and relayed back that he, Lincoln, and Beck, with two fireguards, would be out at 6 a.m. with pack frames and other equipment in order to pack out all the essentials. We all arrived at the site of the grizzly about 7 a.m., and with a rope and several strong men pulled the bear out of the trees.

Beck was busy with his tapeline, measuring the skull, paws, chest circumference, and much more. Lincoln seemed preoccupied staring at the grizzly. After a few minutes he went to his packsack and extracted a fifth of Old Fitzgerald whisky, pulled the cap, and took a drink. Still looking at the bear he exclaimed, "Christ! What a bear," and pushed the bottle my way saying, "Have a drink." He walked around the bear, again extracted the cap, had another drink, and exclaimed, "God! What a bear. Have another one." Not wanting to offend him, I took a sip. Then we all went to work.

Most everyone was rather amazed at the performance of taxidermist Beck. In very short order we had the hide and head on a packboard and all the bones and other essentials packed. The bullet had severed a section of the aorta artery from the top of the heart, and bullet fragments were found in the right lung, which exhibited signs of considerable hemorrhaging. Yet the grizzly traveled more than 400 yards before collapsing.

Later we were provided this information about the bear from Beck's calculations: shoulder height 52 inches, hind foot 12.5 inches; length, nose to tail vertebra, 89 inches; weight approximately 816 pounds. The skull was the largest recorded grizzly in the lower 48 states in 1943 and the second largest ever measured from Wyoming by the Boone & Crockett Club. It was not registered with Boone & Crockett because of where and how it originated. The bear was shot from a distance of 156 yards. Beck said his weight estimate probably was accurate within 20 pounds. For comparison, below is a chart showing the measurements of Yellowstone grizzly bears weighed by Dave Condon at the Fishing Bridge Incinerator in 1942, compared to the grizzly I shot in 1943.

GRIZZLY BEARS WEIGHED BY DAVE CONDON AT FISHING BRIDGE INCINERATOR IN 1942						Bob Murphy's Grizzly
Date Killed	7/8/1942	7/10/1942	7/11/1942	7/11/1942	7/12/1942	6/16/1943
Sex	Male	Female	Female	Female	male	male
Tip of nose/end of last vertebrae	76 1/2"	67"	68"	66"	77"	89"
Elbow to tip of toe	22"	22"	17 1/2"	16 1/2"	20"	26"
R hind ft-width	6"	5 3/4"	5"	4 1/2"	6"	6 1/2"
R hind ft-length	10"	9 1/2"	7 1/2"	7"	11 1/2"	12 1/2"
R front ft-width	6 1/2"	5 1/2"	4 1/2"	4"	6"	6 1/2"
R front ft-length	7 1/2"	6"	5"	5"	9"	9 1/2"
Head width between ears	9 3/4"	10"	9"	10"	10 1/2"	11 1/2"
Head length	14 1/2"	13"	15"	14"	12"	19"
Hgt--front shoulder	39 1/2"	43"	39"	33"	41"	52"
Hgt--rear hip	38"	34"	37"	31"	36"	50"
Girth—neck	32"	30"	29"	28"	34"	34 1/2"
Girth—chest	51"	52"	55"	45"	55"	58"
Weight	497	346	340	375	590	*

* Although Beck estimated the weight at 816 + or - 20 pounds this system of weight estimate can be questioned, but regardless, this bear was obviously a very large grizzly.

Both of the bears killed in 1943 were subsequently mounted and exhibited at the Los Angeles County Museum. The exhibit was captioned, "Honeymooning in Yellowstone," and featured a painting of Yellowstone Lake in the background.

This was a yesterday activity. Today some of us probably would be subjected to considerable criticism for such an undertaking, but at the time, such collections were viewed as giving an educational opportunity to the public.

ISLAND BOUND BEARS

SOMETIMES things got a little complicated, and in early June 1953, a telephone call from Sherman Jones at the Yellowstone Company Boat Dock in front of Lake Hotel kind of fit that category. "You guys got a grizzly with three cubs on Stevenson Island. She chased us off the dock over there this late afternoon." The island was roughly two miles from the Lake Hotel docks.

The Yellowstone Company guide boats frequently, in fishing Yellowstone Lake, stopped at Stevenson Island to have a fish fry for their guests. In this instance Jones had set up his barbecue, put some charcoal under the grill, and ignited the coals. He then noticed a grizzly bear emerging from the woods, followed by three small cubs. She appeared "hell bent" for the dock. Jones picked up the barbecue and dumped the live coals into the lake, and they all scrambled into the boat and backed away from the dock. The mother bear came right onto the dock and sniffed around where the people had been standing. Jones' comment, "She appears to be one hungry bear." This very elongated, narrow island obviously didn't have an abundance of food for a mother bear with three cubs.

At Lake Ranger Station, District Ranger DeLyle Stevens headed a discussion to develop a plan to remove the bears. We had a wooden flat-topped barge that could be towed by a patrol boat, and presumably we could load a bear trap on it and float the unit over to the island. At park headquarters

Chief Ranger Otto Brown and Assistant Chief Ranger Stan McComas were interested in this unusual venture and said they would come to Lake Ranger Station the next morning.

Moving the barge to the island worked out as planned. We unloaded the trailer trap onto the dock and backed it off to a grassy spot. We baited the trap with a ham bone and brown sugar. We searched briefly for the bears, but not wanting to tangle with the old gal, we departed the area.

A little more than an hour after we got back to the ranger station, Bill Dunn, manager of the nearby fish hatchery, called. He said that in coming by boat from Clear Creek and passing Stevenson Island, he saw a bear in the trap.

There was a flurry of activity to gather what we thought was needed in equipment: three large garbage cans with lids, two long bamboo poles with sash cord rigged to snare the cubs, sacks, and small canvas tarps. The next morning off we went and found an unhappy mother bear in the trap. Six of us searched various locations for the cubs, but no cubs! We went to the southeast end of the island and spread out about 50 yards apart and combed the island, which at most was about 300 yards wide. Still no cubs. There was a rocky point off the northwest end of the island that one had to wade about 100 yards of open water to reach. Finally we spotted the cubs out among those rocks.

Three of us took the bamboo poles and three canvas bags and waded toward the rocky point. The others put off in the boat and headed out to the point. Well, as we waded out toward the rocks, the three squalling cubs started swimming across the lake like three river otters. The boat, with the three garbage cans in readiness, pulled alongside the cubs. Otto Brown reached down, grabbed one of the cubs by the nape of the neck, and lifted him out of the water—whereupon the cub turned upside down and nailed Otto's wrist with its sharp teeth. Otto shook him off and made other plans.

The cubs came back near the rocky point and we went into action with the cane poles. One cub came close to shore and I missed snaring him. A tall seasonal ranger went into the water up to his shoulders and snared one little guy. He managed to get him about four feet from shore when the cub wiggled out of the snare, and all the cubs again took off across the lake.

This time Brown wore a long leather glove on his catching hand plus some padding taped on his forearm. The boatmen eventually lifted all three cubs from the water and deposited each one in a garbage can and tied down the lids.

Back at the Lake Dock we unloaded everything, including the trailer trap, and headed for Hayden Valley and up the fire road toward Mary Mountain to release the bears. Our plan was to set out the three garbage cans in a line, park a pickup next to them for protection, and tip the garbage cans over to release the cubs. At the same time, the pickup towing the trailer trap, with a ranger on top to lift the release gate, would approach the garbage cans and release the mother grizzly. A sure-fire plan! Well, the mother bear went north, and the cubs, apparently more frightened by the running mother than by us, went up the road and turned south. A very disappointed group watched the mother bear go over an open ridge to the northwest nearly one mile away. The cubs headed west on the road and turned south through the open grassland and were about a half mile away when last seen.

That evening just before sundown, my wife and I drove back to Hayden Valley and parked about 300 yards east of the release sight. We glassed the area with binoculars for nearly a half hour. My wife suddenly grabbed my arm and said, "There she is!" Off to the northwest in the exact location where she earlier disappeared came the mother grizzly, backtracking her original route. We quietly waited and she finally came back to the fire road about 50 yards west of the release site. The mother bear had her nose to the ground like a bird dog and traveled west on the route the cubs had taken. Exactly where the cubs turned south, she turned south. She wandered from left to right just like a bird dog, losing the scent and then returning to it. She last disappeared in the same location where we had last seen the cubs heading south. Upon returning to the Lake Ranger Station we revealed our observation and everyone cheered.

This grizzly female, being pregnant, most likely wandered across to the island over frozen ice in December. Two locations were found on the island where she had dug under logs and could have given birth to the three cubs.

A BEAR, A BOY, AND A TREE

THERE had been a thunderstorm over Yellowstone Lake with intermittent rain showers on this day in late August of 1955. The clouds had partially cleared as I drove the government pickup into the parking area at the rear of Yellowstone Lake Ranger Station. Dick Peterson was the seasonal park ranger tending the office that day. The District Ranger, DeLyle Stevens, was at the Mayo Clinic for a physical checkup and I was acting District Ranger.

As I entered the office, Dick greeted me in his usual cheerful manner and I sat down. We talked briefly about recent events. Momentarily the phone rang and Dick answered it, listened for a few moments, turned my way and said, "It's for you."

Immediately I was aware that this was a rather frantic call from the lady manager at the Fishing Bridge cafeteria. "Mr. Murphy, a bear has a boy cornered up in a tall tree—get over here right away!"

Pete asked, "What's that all about?" I told him and said we had better get over there right away. "While I get a rifle, call Ranger John Harmon at the Fishing Bridge Ranger Station and find out what he knows about the incident." As I came back with the 30-06 rifle and a box of cartridges, Pete said there was no answer at the ranger station.

We immediately headed on the road north about 1.5 miles

and turned east, crossing Fishing Bridge. Suddenly we noticed quite a crowd of people among the large lodgepole pine trees and willows between the west end of Fishing Bridge Campground and the Yellowstone River at its outlet of Yellowstone Lake. We drove on east and entered the campground, where we were met by a seasonal ranger and a National Park Service maintenance man. They briefed us and said Senior Seasonal Ranger John Harmon had taken a youth injured by a bear to the nurse's office over at the housekeeping cabins. His action resulted in the phone call that we received at Lake Ranger Station. We were then joined by another ranger who had walked in from the Fishing Bridge Cabin area. He informed me that ranger Harmon was transporting the injured youth to the hospital at Mammoth Hot Springs, 50 miles away.

Immediately we all went down among the large trees where the crowd was assembled. My first observation was a youth high in a large lodgepole pine. He was about seven or eight feet from the top, where the tree was only about three inches in diameter. The youth had a rather environmentally excessive grip on that portion of the tree. Then I noticed a fairly large brown black bear straddled on one of the larger limbs, hugging the tree, moaning, clicking her teeth, and slobbering—only 10 or 12 feet below the youth.

People had been throwing stones and sticks at the bear, which only served to drive it farther up the tree—not a logical conclusion to the problem. I moved back from the tree some distance where I could talk to the youth. The rangers and maintenance man started moving the crowd of people out of the area so that the atmosphere could settle down a bit.

As I started talking to the youth, I was immediately aware he was fearful of what I intended to do with the rifle. He stated, "Mr. Ranger, I think I can jump out of the tree." I replied, "God no, didn't attempt to jump, the ground is very rocky and you'll be seriously injured. I'm not going to shoot. We'll try to let things settle down a bit and maybe the bear will come down out of the tree."

Everyone had vacated the area, with one ranger about 200 yards toward the campground and another ranger about 200 yards toward the Fishing Bridge road to keep people from coming into the area. I moved about 75 yards northwest among some other trees where I could see both the bear and the youth and kept up a conversation with him in a subdued voice. The youth's replies seemed a bit disturbing to the bear. In about ten minutes the bear moved down about eight feet to a larger limb and there she sat.

The youth told me that earlier the people told him to come down the tree and try kicking the bear on the nose. I thought that's a pretty gutsy venture but more so when the youth stated, "The bear chewed off both of my rubber heels." This kid was wearing ankle-top shoes and it crossed my mind that it was a wonder the bear didn't jerk him clear out of the tree. Again he asked if I thought it advisable to jump, saying, "That bear is never going to come out of the tree." I again gave him a very negative reply. I asked him how seriously his friend was hurt. He said he didn't know because he was busy climbing up this tree and couldn't see his friend or the ranger that later came to the site, but he heard his friend scream and knew he was hurt. He told me his name was Joey Pinter and they were both from Wyoming and he was staying with his friend's folks over in the Fishing Bridge housekeeping cabins.

We surmised the parents were probably over at the nurse's office or maybe the ranger wouldn't let them come down here, especially with the bear in the tree. He then told me there was another, smaller bear around somewhere.

I had been keeping this youth occupied for about half an hour and I didn't have tranquilizers to immobilize the bear. People watching from the campground and road may have thought I was waiting for the bear to die of old age. I finally told the youth that I may have to soon shoot the bear, and if I did shoot, to hold his position. I'd noticed previously that a bear will continue to try to climb up a tree even though critically wounded.

Steam was rising from the willows and grass due to the earlier rain shower. I decided I'd better get this over with, so I held just off the bear's front elbow and pulled the trigger. The bear trembled and I noticed her muscles relaxing and her hug on the tree start to loosen. She was about to fall from the tree.

I looked at the base of the tree and what did I see? Not eight feet from the base, there was a bespectacled guy wearing a light trench coat and carrying a fishing pole, a camera, light meter, pencils, and other little items. I quickly looked at the bear and she was coming down. I drew in a deep breath to scream at this guy, but he was already in full flight. That trench coat was sticking straight out horizontally. There were a couple of old rotten logs on the ground in the direction he was heading. He cleared the first one but stubbed his toe on the second log and crash-landed on the other side. First there were eyeglasses, light meter, pencils, and camera in the air. Then the trench coat continued to float over his upper body. Most of his belongings eventually came down to earth, and in spite of my concern for the boy and the bear, I was about to "crack up" with laughter. I did manage to keep it inside me and in an instant I was over at the base of the tree with my rifle pointed at the dying bear.

I was about to turn my thoughts to coaxing the youth down from the tree when *jeez*, I looked around on the opposite side of the tree and there was the kid already, peeking around and looking at the dead bear. I made immediate inquiry concerning his welfare. "You feel OK—were you injured in any manner, hurting anywhere on your body?" "Naw, just really scared." I noticed he was scanning the ground near the base of the tree and he picked up one of the rubber heels from his shoes. He verbally exhibited a bit of pride that he was able to kick that bear in its face and not be injured. "Lucky," he said.

I talked to the boy as we walked back to my pickup. There we were joined by one of the rangers who had been instructed to bring the youth to the nurse's office for a checkup. We were all concerned about what had happened and how the chain of events led to two youths' efforts to climb into separate trees to escape an enraged bear.

The following day I paid a visit to Ranger John Harmon to learn other details and the extent of injuries to the youth he had taken to the hospital. Harmon, a coach at Texas A&M University the rest of the year, possessed a real southern drawl and always exhibited a degree of wit in his conversations. In our closing conversation he stated, "Murphy, how many times have you shot a bear out of a tree with a boy up in the very top. Gaud, this is unreal, isn't it?" I replied, "First time, John, glad it wasn't more serious." A few days later, the *Billings Gazette* had the following story, datelined August 28, 1955.

"Rock Springs, Wyoming - Delamar Normington of Superior says he still like bears despite the mauling he received from one in Yellowstone National Park. Normington, transferred to a hospital here from one at Mammoth Hot Springs, told how he lost his race up a tree to a 385-pound black bear.

"Normington and a friend, Joey Pinter, 14, also of Superior, were gathering wood near Fishing Bridge Camp in the park when the Pinter boy thought he heard strange noises. A bear ambled out of the woods and took after Pinter. The youth made it to the top of a nearby tree, out of reach of the animal, but Normington wasn't so lucky. He was still climbing when the bear caught him and badly chewed and clawed the muscles in the youth's legs and thighs.

"The boys' shouts drew fishermen to the scene. They attempted to beat off the bear with sticks. It turned to attack them, but two rangers appeared and shot the bear."

As in many such incidents, there was a story behind the story. The Normington family, accompanied by Joey Pinter, had rented a cabin at Fishing Bridge. One could purchase firewood for the cabins' wood-burning stoves, but at the time it was permissible to gather down or dead wood. So the two youths, with a single-bit axe and a black German shepherd on a leash, left the cabin area, crossed the Fishing Bridge road, and traveled into the woods west of the campground. Holding onto the dog evidently inhibited their wood-gathering efforts, so they turned it loose.

Shortly the two boys realized the dog was absent, and they heard it barking some distance to the south, which they investigated. The dog had treed a one-year-old brown black bear cub. They started back when they heard noises in the adjoining trees and the apparent mother bear charged them. The first encounter was between the mother bear and the dog, with the bear driving the dog from the immediate site. The bear then turned and charged Delamar Normington, who was holding the axe. He swung the axe at the bear, dropped it, and ran for a large tree. The dog had returned and was nipping at the bear. Joey Pinter picked up the axe, just sort of threw it at the bear, and he, too, ran for a large tree and started climbing.

The bear then charged Delamar, grabbing his hip and dragging him out of his tree onto the ground. This bite took a deep chunk of flesh out of his thigh and ripped his jeans about four inches wide down to the bottom hem. The bear was chewing or clawing on his legs when the dog, more enraged, started chewing on the bear. Fortunately for Delamar, this time the dog got the better of the bear and succeeded in driving it away. Unfortunately for Joey, the dog chased the bear up the same tree Joey was in.

Someone had called the Fishing Bridge Ranger Station about the situation and Ranger John Harmon and another ranger arrived. Due to the seriousness of Delamar Normington's wounds, they immediately transported him to the nurse's office.

Later I asked Harmon of his concern for the youth in the tree with the bear below him. "You know Murph, I saw the bear in the tree but didn't, with all the excitement, realize there was a kid in that tree until we were about to transport Normington from the area. That's why I sent someone to the cafeteria to call you.

"He must have been scared as hell because he initially never said a word, so I didn't know he was up there for some time. So I just delegated that problem to someone else, HA!"

GRIZZLY VERSUS HORSE

PELICAN Springs Patrol Cabin was located in large, open, grassland bordered by pine forest. John French, a native of Gardiner, Montana, was the National Park Service fireguard at this location in July 1945. Northeast of Pelican Valley was Pelican Cone Fire Lookout, which was also manned by a park service employee, primarily for forest fire detection.

French's responsibilities consisted of packing supplies and water to the lookout, clearing and maintaining trails, and suppressing small, lightning-caused forest fires. He was, therefore, in constant use of his saddle horse "Buddy" and his packhorse "Pat."

He related the following events: "I had spent three days packing supplies and doing minor repairs at Fern Lake Patrol Cabin about 15 miles to the north. It had been prearranged that I would meet Ranger Russ Noah from Lake Ranger Station on Thursday about 12 miles to the south at the end of the fire road where Pelican Creek enters Pelican Valley. Noah was bringing in supplies for the lookout and Pelican Springs Cabin about three miles to the east.

"I got up early, made breakfast, cleaned up the cabin, and rounded up my two horses. It was starting to rain as I departed the cabin with very dark and threatening clouds in the direction I was heading. As I rode out of the pine forest into Pelican Valley, Noah was there with his pickup and the supplies. By this time it was raining heavily and there were several close lightning strikes. My packhorse, Pat, was very nervous and hopping around, so I hurriedly placed a shovel deep in the ground and wrapped his halter rope around the upright handle. As I hurried to seek shelter in the pickup, a lightning bolt struck the ground about 40 feet away. I was momentarily stunned and all of us were really frightened. Pat reared up backwards, pulled the shovel from the ground, and started running at a full gallop in the general direction of the patrol cabin. The shovel was dragging over the ground, which added to the confusion of the poor horse.

"Russ and I watched in utter amazement as Pat galloped off across the open grassland and disappeared about one mile away. As the sudden storm subsided a bit, I packed all I could on the saddle horse and started heading him in the general direction of the patrol cabin. I followed Pat's trail for a little over two miles and spotted him on the ground, dead (from unknown causes), north of the trail. Sadly I removed the Decker packsaddle and the canvas pack panniers and made a vain attempt to load it on my saddle horse. It was an odd sight with panniers loaded over my riding saddle and sacks tied behind. I then sadly led my saddle horse to the cabin. I arrived at the cabin about 7 p.m., unloaded the horse and put him out on a picket, made supper, and went to bed.

"In the morning I loaded all the supplies I could behind my saddle and started for the lookout. The trail took me near where Pat had died, and as I neared the location I left the trail to see Pat's body. On I went but obviously passed the location and turned back. I rode back toward the cabin for about a half mile and finally spotted the compressed grass where the body had been lying. I rode to the spot and Pat's body was gone!

There was no evidence that any animal had fed on the body, no hair and hide particles scattered around. I then observed very large grizzly bear tracks in the wet ground and a skid path where the bear had dragged this 1000-pound horse toward the pine forest more than 250 yards in the distance. I followed the drag trail up hill into the timber another 100 yards or more. I suddenly realized I was most vulnerable to a bear attack if I should suddenly come upon a large grizzly and his prey.

"I turn around, really confused at the power of a grizzly to drag such a large body so far, and headed for the lookout.

"I was at Pelican Springs Cabin for three months and had previously had no bear problems. However, I suspect grizzly bears did in the night chase the horses off their picket pins."

In 1994 French said, "After 49 years I'd still like to go back and search for some evidence of Pat's bones somewhere in the timber near Pelican Creek."

FIRE LOOKOUT REPAIR

IN the early summer of 1944, repairs were being made to Pelican Fire Lookout due to a winter storm with high winds that had blown off part of the roof. With subsequent snowstorms the interior had also been damaged. Flooring, shingles, shiplap lumber, and about six new windows were needed.

I had six mules and started packing in the material. Bill Mardis was the carpenter and he stayed at the lookout after the first trip. I made about three trips each day. Each evening I would leave my saddle horse and the mules in a meadow near Pelican Creek where I had a pickup truck, and I would drive back to the ranger station at Lake, returning in the morning.

I had just come off the mountain and was caring for the mules and saddle horse. I was driving the picket pin for the horse when I noticed the mules all alert, looking toward the trail that passed our tree-lined location about 200 yards away. Down the trail came a grizzly, walking along rather fast, and he was not looking our way. Suddenly the bear must have gotten our scent because he stopped, reared up on his hind legs, and looked across the open valley with his back to us. In a moment he was down on all fours and running straight in our direction. My saddle horse didn't see him because he was facing away from the bear, but the mules suddenly took off. I grabbed the bridle reins and vaulted into the saddle while my horse was just gently standing there, apparently wondering what had spooked the mules. As I started to thump the horse, he looked back and saw the bear coming at us full speed. The horse took off in high gear. The grizzly was still coming; I thought he must be blind. I was trying to look back and turn the horse. The grizzly finally must have recognized what he was running into because upon my next look in his direction, the grizzly had swapped ends and was heading away from us even faster than he had approached.

I gathered up the mules, unsaddled my horse, and stayed around for a while until they settled down. The next day at the lookout I told Mardis what happened. We both chuckled about the ordeal. When I came off the mountain after my last trip, a stock truck was waiting and everything, including horse and mules, were hauled back to the Lake barn and pasture. No more bears!

GLACIER NATIONAL PARK

WHILE serving as West Side District Ranger at Glacier National Park in the 1950s, one couldn't escape bear problems. I frequently visited Granite Park Chalet and Sperry Chalet and usually would observe grizzly bears. One time at Granite Park, from the veranda in the evening with a telescope, we counted what we believed to be eight grizzly bears. Some were not too distant and two of them were a strong mile away.

There was a ground rule by local rangers that at Granite Park incoming backpackers had to sleep within the chalet's enclosed compound. This wasn't very environmentally exciting, rolling out your sleeping bag next to a woodpile. If a backpacker didn't want to stay within the compound, the closest backpacker campsite was at Bullfrog Lake down off the divide on the east side or down at Packers Roost off the west side. Roy Hutchinson, ranger at Lake McDonald, insisted that backpackers going to Trout Lake have a tent. This latter location was in a cirque in the headwaters of Camas Creek and was prime grizzly bear country. Roy always contended it was better to have a tent torn up than a human body!

Upon retirement and transfer of these rangers, the ground rules were relaxed. A backpacker campsite was established some distance below Granite Park Chalet. The requirement for tents at Trout Lake was abolished, and one could just roll out a sleeping bag on the lakeshore.

Tragically in one night in 1967, two girls were killed by grizzly bears: one at Trout Lake and one near Granite Park Chalet.

It seems we sometimes pay the penalty for demanding our rights for such freedoms! Near these same locations, Bill Yenne, Trail Maintenance Supervisor, and I were packing from Packers Roost on McDonald Creek to Fifty Mountain. Two metal cabins had recently been constructed at Fifty Mountain and we were packing in some interior furnishings.

We traveled up Mineral Creek to its headwaters and headed northwest on the high trail that contours around these high mountains. At one location the trail dipped into a small stream with a heavy alder thicket on each side of the trail. We had just entered this area, riding our saddle horses. I was in front and Bill was behind me leading four pack mules. Suddenly from above the trail a small grizzly, probably a yearling, literally jumped into the trail and stared at us. He let out a woof and darted down the trail, going around a bend out of sight. We all remained stationery and in another instant the apparent mother grizzly came up from below the trail and looked in our direction. Moaning, clicking her teeth, and slobbering, she charged. She came forward with her muzzle close to the ground and pushing her shoulder at us in a sideways approach. We were pecking our saddle horses with spurs to keep them facing the bear. These horses and mules had been in previous bear contacts but likely not with a bear quite as aggressive. I was glad I was riding an old horse, which had probably met more grizzlies on the trail than I had.

The mother bear stopped about 60 feet from us and really

displayed her discontent. She decided to back off but would only move about four to five feet and then turn and face us again. She had repeated this behavior about four times when another grizzly yearling came up behind her from below the trail. When the apparent mother spotted the younger bear, she pounced on it, knocking it down, and pounced on it again. Then they both took off at high speed down the trail and around the bend out of sight. Bill and I held our position and in low voices determined how soon we could safely proceed on the trail.

The mother grizzly hadn't been out of sight more than 10 seconds when back up the trail she came and charged right at us. She was really mad now, more vocal than before. She was trying to bluff us out of the immediate area. Slowly the grizzly pushed herself ever closer. We estimated she was within 35 feet where she finally stopped venting her discomfort. Then, very slowly, she would sort of move backwards a few feet, keeping her full attention on us. She would hold her position for a brief period of time, then repeat a backward movement. Finally, very slowly, she went down the trail, frequently glancing in our direction.

After this was all over we proceeded on our way. Yenne, rather chuckling, said, "How would you like to have been a hiker on foot?"

A GRIZZLY AND MOOSE

IN late August of 1988 most of Yellowstone appeared to be on fire. Due to the wide distribution of the forest fires, much of the backcountry was closed to visitors. A planned horseback trip into the headwaters of the Lamar River was cancelled, so we decided on a trip out of Jackson Hole into the headwaters of the Yellowstone River and the Younts Peak area, in the national forest about 18 miles south of Yellowstone.

In company of Trev and Ellie Povah, my wife and I contacted Bob Johnson, an outfitter out of Kelly, Wyoming. The Povahs owned the Hamilton Stores Concession in Yellowstone. Johnson conducted summer horseback trips in northern Jackson Hole for many years and had a big game hunting camp on Colter Creek just south of the Yellowstone boundary.

Our departure was from Turpin Meadows where the Povahs and my wife and I had trailered our saddle horses. Johnson had two helpers to pack the mules and set up tents and flys at each campsite. We were amazed with the food preparation as each day's food was prepackaged, and Johnson attended the Dutch ovens. All meals were excellent, including deserts, and completed, seemingly, with a minimum of effort.

The first day our route was up the Northfork of the Buffalo River, a tributary of the Snake River. The day was bright and cheerful with only a few sparse white clouds off to the northwest. Smoke from the forest fires could be observed to the north. Around midday we rode through a recent burn that was a slop-over from the Mink Creek Fire. Along the fire lines, recently constructed, some of the large tree stumps were still smoldering.

Our campsite was in the upper reaches of the river drainage in a meadow next to a small stream. My wife and I erected our tent on a grassy area about 50 feet north of the river. Povahs erected their tent about 40 feet north of our tent on the same grassy meadow. Johnson set up his cooking area with fly about 100 yards northeast of our tents. All pack and saddle stock had been unsaddled and tied up, awaiting picketing or hobbles.

We were visiting with the Povahs, having a bit of liquid refreshments. Johnson's two blue heeler dogs were enjoying our attention. Suddenly one of the dogs started growling and looking toward the steep timbered area across the river to the south. Then the other dog took notice of the first dog's attention and, growling, moved toward the riverbank. Almost immediately a large cow moose with her calf trotted out of the timber toward the stream. At first I thought she was just coming down for a drink. However, she really sprinted across the stream with her calf close behind her and then immediately looked back toward the heavily timbered slope. At that moment a large grizzly came running out of the timber toward the creek, obviously zeroed in on the cow and calf. I jumped up and really screamed and waved my arms, moving toward the stream bank. I sure didn't want that grizzly on our side of the stream.

In the meantime the cow and calf sprinted up among the mules and, surprisingly, the mules offered little resistance to their presence. The grizzly stopped short of the stream and kept his attention on the moose. This guy paid minimal attention to me, our tents, or anything in our direction. One of Johnson's wranglers found his 44-magnum revolver and shot in the air. The grizzly turned and walked a few feet back toward the forest but was still looking at the moose and mules, all in a cluster next to the conifer trees. Trev Povah brought me his .357 revolver and I sat down, slowly aimed, and shot into a large rock about six feet behind the grizzly's hind quarters. This evidently pricked him a bit as he hastened forward about 12 feet, looked back, and went up into the forest out of sight.

Needless to say, we had a conference and decided to go on with our chores. The mules were turned loose with a bell mare. Most of the saddle horses were hobbled and two were picketed. I picketed my wife's black appaloosa gelding down by some willows north of our tents about 75 yards. When the mules were turned loose, the cow moose and her calf just stood in the trees, peering out, observing the activities while we had dinner. A little later the cow and calf moose moved down to my wife's saddle horse but stayed in the willows not more than 30 to 40 feet from the horse. Just before dark we noticed the grizzly crossing a snow slide on the steep slope about 350 yards above our campsite. We all slept very lightly that night.

The following day Johnson, Ellie Povah, and I rode to Tri County Lake, a crater lake on top of the Continental Divide mostly above timberline between the Snake River drainage and that of the Yellowstone. When we returned to camp, the cow and calf moose were still close to my wife's saddle horse. In fact Alice said she sort of talked to the moose when she relocated the picket, and they just stared at her and didn't offer to move away.

The next day we broke camp early for a long day crossing the Continental Divide and down Woodard Canyon to the Yellowstone River and up to Boulder Basin. Upon leaving camp we were all a bit sad as the moose and her calf watched from the willows at our campsite. We often wondered if they both survived or if the grizzly came back to resume his chase.

TRAPPING BEARS

THROUGH the years, live trapping of large animals used a variety of devices or structures. A common device was the caged trap, made with a front trap door held in a vertical position above the cage entry. A trigger wire or steel rod extended to the rear of the cage to which bait was securely attached. When the animal being trapped entered the open cage and triggered or pulled on the bait, the front door dropped down and the animal was captured. The cage traps were made of sheet metal and/or steel rods built in a rectangular or box shape. A common one I measured years ago was 36 inches wide across the front, 56 inches in height, 8 feet in length, and mounted on wood skids. The rear end of the trap was a series of vertical, welded, narrowly spaced rods reinforced with horizontal steel rods of equal size. This feature provided ventilation for the captured animal. This caged trap was a transportation problem because the heavy trap plus the trapped animal had to be hand- or machine-loaded onto a truck or other conveyance.

Barrel or culvert traps mounted upon wheeled trailers gradually became the most popular traps, especially for bears. In Yellowstone, the first mention of using a barrel or culvert trap was in 1913 by the U.S. Army in the Grand Canyon area to capture a troublesome bear. The purpose for trapping the bear alive was not clear, perhaps it was sent to a zoo.

In 1923 the National Park Service in Yellowstone described a culvert trap mounted on a rubber-tired carriage. In 1938 I observed a much-improved culvert bear trap mounted on a more modern rubber-tired, two-wheel trailer. In addition to a 48-inch culvert 10 feet in length, the front and rear ends were steel plate with 4-inch round holes cut out for ventilation. The bait trigger rod extended through and under the bottom of the steel front gate. Also, a swivel piece of steel plate rotated over the front of the drop gate so it could not be raised upward, thus preventing the animal from escaping.

There was always a question in trapping bears – where do you locate the trap, especially in areas where park visitors were present. Sometimes it created complications.

One of my first times trapping a black bear with a culvert trap was at the Mammoth Hot Springs dump ground in 1942. The trap was set in the evening and had the bear early the next morning. I hauled him nearly 20 miles to a remote area and released him.

Another ranger borrowed the trap for a troublesome grizzly at Norris Ranger Station. Now when you borrow such an item, especially after catching a grizzly, you wash out the culvert with soap and, preferably, hot water. Later the bear trap was back at Mammoth and a couple of the guys tried to capture a pesky little black bear. They tried enticing bait, ham bone and boned chuck, but no bear would go near the trap. A few days later, I happened to be with the same fellows and they were discouraged. Well, the bottom of the culvert was a mess of sticky stuff. So down at the incinerator we gave the trap a hot-water bath with plenty of soap. But I asked the fellows, "What is that thick stuff on the bottom that doesn't seem to clean up?" We inspected and scraped it up. You know what it was?

Honey: sticky, *grizzly bear-scented* honey. No wonder the little black bear wouldn't go near the trap. After cleaning the trap the guys caught the black bear the very next day. We told the fellow at Norris, "No more honey!" Maybe a bit of brown sugar could be used at the entry to the trap, but no more honey.

In 1954 we had a mother black bear and two small cubs in the Fishing Bridge Campground. This old gal had taken up residence; she was there day and night. We waited until after Labor Day when visitors thinned out. One evening I took over a trailer trap, set it up in a location with few visitors, and baited it. The next morning the mother black bear was in the trap but the two black cubs were high up in a distant, big, lodgepole pine. The lowest tree limbs were about 16 feet above the ground. So I moved the trap with the mother bear next to the base of the tree, hoping the cubs would come down. The next day the cubs were still high in the tree and voicing their discontent.

So we borrowed a trailer trap from Canyon Ranger Station and put it alongside the trap with the mother bear. On day three these cubs were desperately hungry and trying to come down out of the tree. Using thumbtacks I attached about five strips of bacon to the tree as high as I could reach and moved away. One squalling cub came down but, being afraid of me, stayed on the backside of the tree trunk. John Harmon got on top of the empty trap, and he was not totally familiar with all the trigger assembly. The cub came down and swung around the tree trunk under the bacon with total attention to obtaining something to eat – he was starving.

I reached up and grabbed the cub by a hind leg, and he immediately tried to devour part of my right arm. I screamed at John to raise the drop gate on the trap while swinging my arm around and around to keep the cub from feasting on my human flesh. John was pulling on the drop gate with no results. I screamed, "Turn that little swivel metal latch." He did and lifted the drop gate. I then sent that poor little cub thumping to the far end of the trap. He settled down at the inside water container.

The second cub came easier, and soon we had both cubs in one trap and the mother in the other trap. So off we went to Hayden Valley toward Mary Mountain to release them. Often in a release the cubs go one way and the mother bear goes in the opposite direction. Fortunately the cubs jumped out of the trap and remained nearly motionless. The mother bear was released and immediately joined the cubs. They moved away together very slowly, and we hoped she would seek an alternate area away from the campgrounds.

We try to resolve a bear problem in a logical manner with environmental considerations, but logic dissipates when sudden confrontations prompt reactions toward human safety.

A small female grizzly bear frequented the Fishing Bridge Campground in 1954 and became somewhat of a problem due to exhibiting little fear of visitors. This grizzly was trapped on two occasions and released in remote areas. In 1955 she was back in the campground. She was observed in July in the quiet of night and she had three small cubs. This was a bit unusual, and she became more aggressive and bluff charged a couple of visitors.

At Lake Ranger Station as well as Fishing Bridge we were short-handed. So in haste, I took a culvert trap to the Fishing Bridge Campground and placed it about 150 yards east of the campground in the forest, baited the trap, and left the area.

Late that afternoon I was detailed to a forest fire near White Lake, so I asked Ranger Jim Valder to check the trap each morning. Later Jim took a look at the trap and wondered why it had been placed so far outside the campground. He thought that to be more productive, he'd move it into the middle of the campground. He parked the trap at a vacant campsite between a small trailer and a tent, hoping to expedite the live capture of this female grizzly.

I came off the forest fire in the evening about three days later. About 9 p.m. we got a telephone call from Fishing Bridge Ranger Station stating that a grizzly bear had bluff-charged several people. There was a cub in the trap and the mother grizzly was most aggressive. People were leaving in haste and scared to death of this roaming mother bear.

I immediately got ready to go to Fishing Bridge. Ranger Jim Valle was on "days off," so a seasonal ranger joined me and we drove to the Fishing Bridge Ranger Station. The parking lot was full of visitors seeking advice from the resident ranger on a more peaceful location to spend the night. We talked at some length with the ranger and a few of the park's concerned visitors.

On of the concerned people was a cowboy-type from Green River, Wyoming. He was very informative and related in detail what happened during the evening: "I was camped over on the northeast section of the campground." This loop has about 24 campsites. "I saw the mother bear with her three cubs going down to the southwest section where the bear trap was parked. Shortly I heard some loud voices, a woman screaming and later more hollering. After about 10 minutes the mother bear came by my campsite with two cubs, charging toward a couple of visitors and pushing her two cubs across the highway and into the forest beyond. A guy from another campsite had investigated the disturbance and hurriedly related that there was a cub bear in the trap and the mother bear had bluff-charged several people down there and a man had been injured in a fall over a guardrail in avoiding the mother bear."

"I bet there was some soiled underwear among those poor people," the man said. "Later I observed three other campers pulling out. This mother bear came back into the campground and proceeded down to the bear trap. Shortly she started cleaning house, charging several people, and scaring the hell out of them. Visitors were packing up, hollering, yelling and driving away. Now this mother bear was widening her charges and getting closer to my location. I didn't have any argument with this bear so the wife and I hitch up and head for the ranger station."

We spent quite a bit of time helping the stressed visitors and finally pried the resident seasonal ranger away and into the government pickup. It was getting late and we needed to check out the campground and the bear trap. We three rangers climbed into the pickup and proceeded very slowly into the campground. I had a 30-06 rifle and hoped I didn't have to use it. This was the height of the summer season and the campground had been nearly full before the mother bear went on her rampage. The east end of the campground had been totally vacated. I couldn't believe what I saw. In their haste to depart, campers left ice chests, food lockers, a table, folding chairs and many other items.

We stopped a short distance from the bear trap and pondered what to do. Do we possibly release the cub, hoping the mother bear and cubs will leave the area? So the Fishing Bridge ranger exited the pickup and headed for the trap to release the cub.

When the ranger was about a third of the way to the trap, the mother showed up on the run from the opposite direction and the ranger rushed back into the pickup. Where did the mother bear come from? Why didn't we see her when we drove up? We waited in the pickup, hoping the mother bear would wander away. We thought maybe we could drive the pickup toward the trap and move back the mother bear long enough to release the cub. Well, this mother bear changed our plans real quick. She charged the pickup head on, beating and scratching the hood. We were afraid she would demolish the headlights. Then she darted toward the trap and then charged back to the front of the pickup.

It was nearly midnight and we didn't have an immediate solution. The mother bear was really in a rage now, and on her third return from the trap to the pickup, the rifle barked and, unfortunately, this mother bear ceased to exit. A sad event! The three cubs were eventually sent to a zoo with some tentative plans for reintroduction into the wild. Naturally we didn't feel good about this ending, but I guess the lesson learned was don't mix bear traps with visitors – it doesn't work.

Sometimes we were introduced to bear problems that exceeded our expectations. The mess hall building in back of Lake Hotel had some periodic problems with mostly black bears. This facility was a kitchen and dining area for hotel employees. It was also a meat-cutting location for both the hotel and employee mess operations. In years past it occasionally attracted black bears due to meat scraps being tossed out to attract bears for guest observations. However, such contributions to bears had not been permitted recently. Still, bears on occasion were attracted to the location, possibly due to cooking odors and other features that attract bears.

It was the first day of September in 1955 and my wife and I were alone at Lake Ranger Station. I received a late afternoon telephone call from the Lake Hotel manager that a large black bear had been hanging around the mess hall building, damaging the screen door, and was evidently trying to gain entrance to the building.

I took over a culvert trap, parked it near the building but to one side, and baited it. I then contacted the hotel desk and requested that they call the Lake Ranger Station as soon as possible if a bear was captured.

Shortly after 7 a.m. the next morning, the assistant manager called and said there was a large black bear in the trap. I took off and with no problems, hitched onto the trailer trap, headed out the East Entrance Road, over Sylvan Pass, down the east side about four miles, and released the bear. He immediately headed down the hill and the last I saw of him, he was near Middle Creek, a new and, I hoped, accommodating territory.

I went back to Lake Ranger Station, cleaned the trap, and reset it in back of the hotel to the side of the mess hall. It was about 11:30 a.m. so I went to have lunch with my wife at the ranger station.

At about 1:30 p.m., the hotel called, "You got another bear, a brown one." Now my wife, Alice, was curious, "What are you trying to do, catch all the bears in Yellowstone?" So we both went over to the mess hall where she helped me hitch up the bear trap. We headed toward Sylvan Pass and the East Entrance. Without incident, we released a medium-sized female black bear high in the Absaroka Mountains inside the park. This bear jumped out of the trap, turned around, and acted like she wanted to reenter the trap. My wife said, "Maybe she wants a ride back to Lake."

We reset the culvert trap alongside the mess hall. It was close to 5:30 p.m. so we went to eat dinner. At about 7 p.m. we got a call from the hotel that we had another bear in the trap. So Alice and I went over and hitched onto the trap. It was an average-sized black bear. It was going to be a long day! We went back over Sylvan Pass and released this bear in a parking area where we had released the last bear. We headed home. It was dark as we drove along the shore of Yellowstone Lake, and we left the bear trap in the parking lot behind the ranger station. My wife commented, "Got enough for one day?"

About four days later my old buddy at Pahaska Lodge down the road from the East Entrance called me. He said, "Where in the hell are all these bears coming from? I had a big black bear on my back porch yesterday morning, real early, and this morning a brown black bear was on my porch." Yes, I had probably contributed to the increase in his bear population. We had also taken a couple of bears over that way in July. Years later I confessed to the total.

SUMMATIONS

IN coping with wildlife situations, we are sometimes hesitant to reveal our past, both bad and good. We have significantly changed our attitudes to a more protective nature, based on scientific and environmental concerns. Through more recent research we have learned to recognize methods of wildlife management that are beneficial to both the wildlife and the public. However, past practices are part of the record, and I cannot shun these experiences. I can only explain that attitudes are appreciably changed in today's environment.

Many times I recall incidents that were observed with a degree of humor and others that were damaging to property and humans. Some incidents reflected the problems of humans and bears, sometimes uninformed or stupid people. Other times we wondered why some bears reacted so aggressively and threatened humans without just cause—in the eyes of the human. But bears don't think like humans, so we humans have to be cautious in extending our reasoning to them.

Why do bears resort to activities that are not fully explainable to wildlife authorities or to the public?

In 1939 Park Naturalist Wayne Replogle reported on a motorboat trip from West Thumb to the southeast corner of Yellowstone Lake. He observed a grizzly bear running southward along the shoreline of Wolf Point and entering the forest. Further on, he noted a black bear swimming toward Dot Island more than one mile away. As the boat approached the black bear, it started swimming north and away from the island. The bear was followed for nearly five miles until it reached the north shore, where it climbed the bank and fled into the forest. Was it escaping the grizzly or just on an endurance swim?

In 1944 I was operating a motorboat going to the Southeast Arm of Yellowstone Lake. Between Dot Island and Frank Island my passengers and I noted an object in the water. As we approached, the object turned out to be a black bear. He was several miles from the mainland and more than a mile from either of the islands. The bear appeared to just be playing in the lake. He would roll over, partly submerge, and then swim around in a circle. We observed the bear from about 100 yards for more than 20 minutes. The bear exhibited no concern to our presence and when last observed was enjoying his swim and not really heading for either of the islands.

In 1944 I was stationed at the Thorofare Ranger Station in the extreme southeast corner of Yellowstone until mid November. During the late summer and early fall we covered many trails, especially during the hunting season outside the park. Others had commented about seeing the track of a 3-toed grizzly bear in Mountain Creek. This grizzly bear would come down the Mountain Creek Trail about every six to seven days, leaving his 3-toe print in the dusty trail. No one ever, to my knowledge, observed this track anywhere else. I, nor others, ever observed his paw prints going up Mountain Creek. What wide circle did this bear travel? Where did he go? And why no 3-toe tracks in any of the other numerous trails?

Grizzly bear feeding habits might tell us where to observe grizzly bears and/or where to avoid them. There were times of the year when we could expect grizzly bears or even black bears in certain localities.

An elk calving ground was near Indian Pond (Squaw Lake) east of Fishing Bridge and north of Yellowstone Lake. In early June 1944, I was on horseback along the fringe of the forest when, with no warning, a female grizzly charged out of the trees. My saddle horse about had a heart attack but I finally got him facing the bear. I guess we bluffed the bear. Very slowly she left when her two cubs came forth. I hesitated to check the area but did find the legs and head of a calf elk. The following year we monitored this area in late May and early June. There were 45 to 48 cow elk in this calving area, no bulls. A mother grizzly with two yearling cubs showed up for an extended period of time. Searching on horseback, we observed where nine calf elk were killed, and three times bears were on these kills. Near the end of calving season, six elk calves had evidently survived and were traveling with their mothers. Elk calving grounds, especially in the northern section of Yellowstone, were areas to use extreme caution in approaching grizzly bears. The same was true of mountain streams when cutthroat trout were spawning. In the fall we might encounter grizzly bears in the whitebark pine forests digging up squirrel caches of pine nuts. But I did not observe any appreciable aggression by these bears in comparison to grizzlies on kill sites of elk or other wildlife.

I often wonder why individual bears, especially grizzlies, resort to certain destructive activities.

In late summer of 1943, someone reported a probable bear break-in at the Cabin Creek Patrol Cabin off the upper end of the Southeast Arm of Yellowstone Lake. Two of us took a boat across the lake to the mouth of Beaver Dam Creek and walked about three miles to the cabin. On the outside there were deep claw marks around the window shutters and the entry storm door. This cabin was cut into the uphill slope, which made it easy to access the roof. The bear had clawed and chewed an entry into the cabin through the roof. When we entered the cabin, there really wasn't much disturbed. The two mattresses, several blankets, and other bedding were in a pile in the middle of the floor. These items had been suspended over a long pole, down and parallel from the ridge log. This procedure was taken to prevent mice or other vermin from damaging the bedding. Nothing was otherwise disturbed, so we suspected the bear caused the mattresses and blankets to fall to the floor, prompting the bear to depart in great haste and not return.

In early 1944, some fishermen reported the Lower Blacktail Cabin broken into, probably by a bear. Paul Hoppe (pack master) and I rode in on horseback and really were amazed as we first observed the cabin. The cook stove was out in the yard. The storm door made of 2 x 8 planks was wide open, even though the heavy door had been secured to the entry frame by a spike through an eyebolt. The bear had likely pulled up the spike and opened the door. (Some cabins were not locked at that time.) The inner door of more fragile plywood was completely torn from its frame and in pieces on the floor. The metal wall cabinets were ripped from the wall and on the floor. The table and chairs were damaged, pushed into a corner of the room. The Coleman lantern was crushed on the floor. Stovepipes were damaged and scattered about and soot was spread over about a third of the floor.

Paul and I put some things in temporary order, awaiting

other employees to rehab the entire cabin. Our most difficult task was getting the cooking stove back into the cabin. It was a bit wider than the doorway. As we were trying to drag it into the cabin we noticed that a section of the wooden doorstop about two inches wide was knocked out about six inches higher than the top of the stove. Our question: How in the hell did that bear remove that stove from the cabin? He would have had to lift it up to where he knocked out a small section of the doorstop to make enough room for it to go through.

In September of 1944 Clyde Gilbert, an outfitter out of Jardine, Montana, called park headquarters to report a bear had broken into the Crevice Ranger Station, which was inside the park about three miles above Mr. Gilbert's place.

District Ranger Hugh Ebert and I drove up to Gilbert's hunting headquarters. There was no one home so we drove on up the very primitive road to the ranger station. We viewed the two-room station from the outside and walked around it, noting only a heavy plank window shutter that was open. The window was broken out and the entire frame removed. We unlocked the entry door and viewed the mess inside. Glass fragments were scattered all over the floor. Two metal wall cabinets were torn from the walls and their doors were open or broken off. Rice, beans, and dried foods were scattered about. The cook stove was still upright but rotated about 90 degrees. The ceiling showed bear claw marks in several locations. The Coleman lantern that had been hanging from the ceiling was beaten into a C-shape and left against the far wall. The water bucket was beaten up, and broken plates and cookware were scattered about the room. There were claw marks on the door and casing leading to the wood storage area.

Oddly, the sleeping room adjacent to the cooking and dining

room apparently wasn't touched by the bear. The mattresses, blankets, and other bedding were in order and hanging on the long pole from the ceiling. The AM radio, table, and chair were not disturbed. There was no door between these rooms, just an opening.

There wasn't much we could do, so after putting tables and chairs upright and sweeping up the glass and broken dishes, we departed. A short time later a government carpenter replaced the broken window and replaced the wall cabinets. I arrived about a week later and cleaned up the remainder and scrubbed the floors. The first week in October, I arrived at the ranger station with two horses and baled hay. I was there till late January, primarily for the Montana elk-hunting season, and never saw a bear track during my travels along the park boundary. I did wonder about that cabin bear, obviously a grizzly, and wondered what I'd do if he showed up during the middle of the night.

Sometimes we learn things about bears even in odd locations, and one of my favorite places was the Trout Creek Dump Ground. Its location was off the road between Grand Canyon and Fishing Bridge, about three miles up the Mary Mountain fire road. It was a deep, dry ravine where garbage and other material were deposited. It was the last location in Yellowstone where a concentration of bears could be viewed, but not by the public. A locked gate kept it very private. The Canyon bear feeding ground was closed in 1941, but the Trout Creek Dump continued for a few years until all garbage and other disposable materials were taken outside of the park.

One evening I took an official of the U.S. Fish and Wildlife Service to the Trout Creek Dump. We parked our vehicle on a grassy ledge above the dump and viewed bears coming and going.

As part of the site's operation, the dumped material was frequently covered with soil, and it was most interesting to see how bears could locate a food item and dig down through the dirt to extract it. Frequently a few black bears, usually only three or four, would come to the dump early. As the number of grizzly bears increased, the black bears reluctantly departed. Once, 59 grizzlies were counted at the dump at the same time.

Large male grizzlies dominated the location. Females with cubs were more timid and some would leave when outnumbered by the males. A few female grizzlies would leave their cubs on a high bank opposite from where we were parked. The females would then cautiously go down to the dump and search for food.

I visited the Trout Creek Dump on a number of occasions, including twice, I believe, with the Craighead brothers in looking for marked bears during their research.

Such an opportunity to view grizzly bears in such numbers became rather contagious. My wife and I visited the site a number of times, sometimes with friends but usually on our own. We quickly learned to identify individual bears, some by color, some by sex, several by behavior, especially dominance, and others by facial or body construction. It was interesting to notice the direction they traveled, usually from the west, but one time we observed a large grizzly that was dripping wet, apparently from crossing the Yellowstone River three miles away. We witnessed some real battles between large males. Some were intense enough to send the defeated away, not to return again that evening.

Then there were characters we named because of their unique behavior. There was a small grizzly bear we named "Jack the Ripper." He was likely a two- or three-year-old. As the dump became crowded with bears, he would climb up on a high bank away from the crowd. There he would look up in the sky, roll around on the grass, look our way, and stare at our vehicle. Then he would dash down the bank toward the dump, increasing his speed, which would alarm the other bears and scatter them from the dump. As the bears returned, "Jack the Ripper" would go back to his perch on the bank. He would repeat this activity about every 20 minutes until his appetite was satisfied.

Another bear was a very large female with two small cubs. She was a very dominant animal, chasing other bears away from her position. She was the exception in that she kept her cubs by her side all the time she was at the dump. We named her cubs "Mike and Ike" as they were very active and well taught by their mother. Several times we witnessed the mother fighting off other grizzly bears. The cubs didn't flee but would stand together, backed up against the mother's hind legs. During one fight one of the cubs even peeked out from between his mother's hind legs. The cubs were two real characters, always in motion and never afraid when their mother was in battle. Most other cubs would flee the dump when their mothers became hostile toward other bears.

There were three or four large male grizzlies that sort of dominated the scene. They would literally clobber other bears, both male and female. Oddly, each of these large bears would take a position in the dump and defend it, but not really fight among themselves.

We frequently stayed at the dump until the evening light failed and then we headed for home, feeling very privileged for the opportunity to view grizzlies up close.

ABOUT THE AUTHOR

ROBERT J. (Bob) Murphy has had a long and distinguished career in the National Park Service. Born in Montana in1918, Murphy worked in Yellowstone National Park while attending Montana State University. He became a seasonal ranger in Yellowstone in 1941 and became a permanent ranger in 1942. He served in Yellowstone until 1957, when he became district park ranger in Glacier National Park, Montana, until 1960.

Murphy's career included positions as chief ranger at Theodore Roosevelt National Park in North Dakota, a management position at Rocky Mountain National Park in Colorado, chief ranger at Wind Cave National Park in South Dakota, and Superintendent at Devil's Tower National Monument in Wyoming. In1964 he was assigned to the National Parks Service director's office in Washington D.C. in Resource Management and Law Enforcement. In 1968 Murphy became superintendent of Death Valley National Park in southern California, and in 1972 he was assigned as superintendent of Lassen Volcanic National Park in northern California. He retired from the National Park Service in 1974.

Upon his retirement, Murphy was awarded the Meritorious Service Award by the Secretary of Interior for outstanding service. He also received a Distinguished Service Award by the Director of the Bureau of Narcotics and Dangerous Drugs, for his participation in their international training programs, and an Award of Appreciation from the President of the Death Valley 49ers.

Murphy and his wife, Alice, live on a ranch south of Livingston, Montana, not far from Yellowstone National Park.Since his retirement, Murphy has worked in real estate and has continued to explore the Yellowstone backcountry, especially on horseback. *Bears I Have Known* is his second book. His first book, *Desert Shadows*, is about the arrest and investigation of the Manson Family in Death Valley, which took place during his tenure there.

BEARS AND BEARS AND BEARS!
Available from Riverbend Publishing

HIKING WITH GRIZZLIES: LESSONS LEARNED
By Tim Rubbert
This book uses photographs of the author's actual bear encounters to dramatically illustrate how to react safely if you meet a bear on the trail. Each encounter teaches important hiking strategies and gives hikers more confidence to enjoy bear country.

"If you are planning to hike through the wilderness, give this book a careful reading—it could very well save your life." —*Midwest Book Review*

"This book is like a first-aid manual for travel in bear country. It could be the best $10.95 you ever spend." —*North American Bear Foundation*

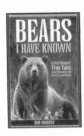

BEARS I HAVE KNOWN
By Bob Murphy
A former park ranger relates his most memorable experiences with bears. These first-hand stories are great entertainment and an inside look at bear management in our national parks. "This is not your average bear book. It's a lifetime's experience in bear country." – *Bozeman Daily Chronicle*

GREAT WYOMING BEAR STORIES
By Tom Reed
The first-ever collection of the best bear tales from all across Wyoming, including Yellowstone and Grand Teton national parks. "An immensely valuable book for understanding and living with Wyoming's bears." —*Laramie Daily Boomerang*

GREAT MONTANA BEAR STORIES
By Ben Long
Maulings, close calls, and even humorous escapades are all found in these stories, complete with discussions about how to hike, camp, and live safely in bear country. "A must-read for all lovers of wilderness." —*Missoulian*